A Concise
User's Guide to
Lotus 1-2-3 Release 3.4

GW00536392

ALSO AVAILABLE

A Concise User's Guide to Lotus 1-2-3 Release 3.4

by

N. Kantaris

and

P.R.M. Oliver

BERNARD BABANI (publishing) LTD.
THE GRAMPIANS
SHEPHERDS BUSH ROAD
LONDON W6 7NF ENGLAND

PLEASE NOTE

Although every care has been taken with the production of this book to ensure that any projects, designs, modifications and/or programs, etc., contained herewith, operate in a correct and safe manner and also that any components specified are normally available in Great Britain, the Publishers and Author(s) do not accept responsibility in any way for the failure (including fault in design) of any project, design, modification or program to work correctly or to cause damage to any equipment that it may be connected to or used in conjunction with, or in respect of any other damage or injury that may be so caused, nor do the Publishers accept responsibility in any way for the failure to obtain specified components.

Notice is also given that if equipment that is still under warranty is modified in any way or used or connected with home-built equipment then that warranty may be void.

© 1993 BERNARD BABANI (publishing) LTD

First Published - June 1993

British Library Cataloguing in Publication Data

Kantaris, Noel
    Concise User's Guide to Lotus 1-2-3
    Release 3.4
    I. Title II. Oliver, Phil
    005.369

ISBN 0 85934 336 7

Printed and Bound in Great Britain by Cox & Wyman Ltd, Reading

ABOUT THIS BOOK

This Concise User's Guide to Lotus 1-2-3 Release 3.4 was written to help existing spreadsheet users upgrade to this latest 3-dimensional spreadsheet from Lotus. Therefore, some basic knowledge of spreadsheet work has been assumed. It is recommended that complete beginners also refer to "A Concise User's Guide to Lotus 1-2-3 Release 2.4" by Noel Kantaris, also published by Bernard Babani (publishing) Ltd.

Lotus 1-2-3 Release 3.4 is a very powerful spreadsheet package that has the ability to work 3-dimensionally with both multiple worksheets and files. It is operated by selecting commands from menus or by writing 'macros' to chain together menu commands. Each method of accessing the package is discussed separately, but the emphasis is mostly in the area of menu-driven command selection. The Wysiwyg interface gives the package the ability to produce excellent professional quality material, as well as the ability to use a mouse. Using a mouse is not mandatory, but its use certainly increases productivity.

Below we list the major enhancements found in Release 3.4 over earlier releases of the package. These are:

- The inclusion of the SmartIcon add-in which allows the user to create and display 'icons' which when selected perform 1-2-3 or Wysiwyg functions.

- The inclusion of 3-D graphs and other graph features, such as the addition of drop shadows.

- The ability to autoload worksheets when you start 1-2-3.

- The ability to specify ranges with the mouse prior to selecting a command.

- The ability to print in landscape mode on all supported printers.

- The ability to 'Trace' all the steps of an executing macro by displaying what is happening in the status line.

- The inclusion in the Translate utility of the ability to convert .WK3 file for use in programs that do not support such file structure.

In addition to the above new features, Release 3.4 supports all the functionality built into Release 3.1+, such as

- The Backsolver add-in that allows the creation of a formula to achieve a desired result by changing one or more variables that affect the result of the formula.

- The Auditor add-in which helps you locate and analyse formulae in your worksheet files.

- The Solver add-in which helps you analyse worksheet data by solving "what-if" type problems.

- The Viewer add-in which allows you to have a look at the contents of files before you retrieve or open them.

Most features of the package (old and new) will be discussed using simple examples that the user is encouraged to type in, save, and modify as more advanced features are introduced. This provides the new user with a set of examples that aim to help with the learning of the most commonly used features of the package, and should help to provide the confidence needed to tackle some of the more advanced features of the package later.

The material in this book is presented on the "what you need to know first, appears first" basis, although the underlying structure of the book is such that you don't have to start at the beginning and go right through to the end. An experienced user can start from any section, as the sections have been designed to be self contained.

Although the book is intended as a supplement to the documentation that comes with the package, at the back of the book, we list all the Lotus functions and macro commands so that it is self contained and can be used as a reference long after you become an expert in the use of the program.

ABOUT THE AUTHORS

Noel Kantaris graduated in Electrical Engineering at Bristol University and after spending three years in the Electronics Industry in London, took up a Tutorship in Physics at the University of Queensland. Research interests in Ionospheric Physics, led to the degrees of M.E. in Electronics and Ph.D. in Physics. On return to the UK, he took up a Post-Doctoral Research Fellowship in Radio Physics at the University of Leicester, and in 1973 a Senior Lectureship in Engineering at Camborne School of Mines, Cornwall, where since 1978 he has also assumed the responsibility of Head of Computing.

Phil Oliver graduated in Mining Engineering at Camborne School of Mines in 1967 and since then has specialised in most aspects of surface mining technology, with a particular emphasis on computer related techniques. He has worked in Guyana, Canada, several Middle Eastern countries, South Africa and the United Kingdom, on such diverse projects as: The planning and management of bauxite, iron, gold and coal mines; rock excavation contracting in the U.K.; international mining equipment sales and technical back up; international mine consulting for a major mining house in South Africa. In 1988 he took up a Senior Lectureship at Camborne School of Mines in Surface Mining and Management.

ACKNOWLEDGEMENTS

We would like to thank colleagues at the Camborne School of Mines for the helpful tips and suggestions which assisted us in the writing of this book.

TRADEMARKS

HP LaserJet and **HP DeskJet** are registered trademarks of Hewlett Packard Corporation

IBM, and **PC-DOS** are registered trademarks of International Business Machines Corporation

Intel is a registered trademark of Intel Corporation

MS-DOS and **WINDOWS** are registered trademarks of Microsoft Corporation

Lotus 1-2-3, Wysiwyg and **Lotus Symphony** are registered trademarks of Lotus Development Corporation

PostScript is a registered trademark of Adobe Systems Incorporated.

CONTENTS

1. INTRODUCTION

Lotus 1-2-3 is a powerful versatile software package which, over the last few years, has proved its usefulness, not only in the business world, but with scientific and engineering users as well. The program's power lies in its ability to emulate everything that can be done by the use of pencil, paper and a calculator. Thus, it is an 'electronic spreadsheet' or simply a 'spreadsheet', a name which is also used to describe it and other similar products. Its power is derived from the power of the computer it is running on, and the flexibility and accuracy with which it can deal with the solution of the various applications it is programmed to manage. These can vary from budgeting and forecasting to the solution of complex scientific and engineering problems.

Lotus 1-2-3 comes in several flavours; Version 2.x (the subject of another book) incorporating Releases 2.2, 2.3 & 2.4, running mainly on IBM XTs and compatibles (computers equipped with Intel's 8086 or 8088 processors). Then, there is Version 3.x (the subject of this, more advanced, book) encompassing Releases 3.1 & 3.4, which require a more powerful computer as a platform, such as an IBM AT, PS/2 or compatible (equipped with Intel's superior 80286, 80386, or 80486 processors). Versions 3.x make use of certain programmable aspects of the 80286 and 80386 processors and, therefore, cannot run on computers with the less powerful processors. All the above versions run under DOS, with Versions 3.1 & 3.4 also capable of running under the Microsoft Windows 3.x environment. In addition, there is Version 1-2-3/W Releases 1.1 & 2.0 which are designed specifically for the Windows environment. Last, but not least, there is Lotus 1-2-3/G, the Presentation Manager version, using a graphical interface front-end, but running under the OS/2 operating system.

This book deals with Lotus 1-2-3 Version 3.x. Spreadsheets built up on previous versions of 1-2-3 can easily be converted to run on Version 3.x, using the 'Translate' option. Downward compatibility, however, is more limited, especially if the 3-dimensional and file linkage facilities have been used in the Version 3.x worksheet. There were no equivalents to these facilities in the pre-2.2 versions.

Package Overview

If you have access to a more powerful PC (equipped with one of the 386 or higher processors), it is well worth upgrading to Release 3.4, which offers many additional options not found in earlier releases. These include:

- The inclusion of the SmartIcon add-in which allows the user to create and display 'icons' which when selected perform 1-2-3, or Wysiwyg functions.

- The inclusion of 3-D graphs and other graph features, such as the addition of drop shadows.

- The ability to autoload worksheets when you start 1-2-3.

- The ability to specify ranges with the mouse prior to selecting a command.

- The ability to print in landscape mode on all supported printers.

- The ability to 'Trace' all the steps of an executing macro by displaying what is happening in the status line.

- The inclusion in the Translate utility of the ability to convert .WK3 files for use in programs that do not support such file structure.

In addition to the above new features, Release 3.4 supports all the functionality built into Release 3.1, & 3.1+, such as:

- The ability to use 3-dimensional worksheet files, each with a maximum of 256 worksheets, of 256 columns by 8,192 rows (subject to available memory).

- The inclusion of Graphical drawing and editing tools and the ability to embed graphs in a worksheet.

- The inclusion of the Backsolver add-in that allows the creation of a formula to achieve a desired result by changing one or more variables that affect the result of the formula.

- The inclusion of the Auditor add-in which helps you locate and analyse formulae in your worksheet files.

- The inclusion of the Solver add-in which helps you analyse worksheet data by solving "what-if" problems.

- The inclusion of the Viewer add-in which allows you to have a look at the contents of files before you retrieve or open them.

The most obvious feature of Version 3.x is the ability to build and work with 3-dimensional worksheets. A .WK3 file when first opened looks like the familiar flat, 2-dimensional worksheet, but you can insert up to 255 other sheets above, or below, it. 1-2-3 formulae and ranges can refer to these multiple sheets, which presents some very exiting possibilities.

The graphical interface included in Version 3.x, is called Wysiwyg, and is implemented as an add-in, which is initially made resident so that it is always operative. If you have a memory problem, however, you can remove it and operate 1-2-3 in text mode. With Wysiwyg invoked, the whole package operates in graphics mode, and a mouse is fully supported.

With version 3.1 and higher, a graph can be shown actually in a worksheet. Once there, a graph can be edited and enhanced. Text, freehand lines and geometric shapes can all be added to it, and .CGM graphics can be imported to further improve presentation.

Installing 1-2-3

All the files on the program discs are compressed, therefore, you must first use the **Install** program, which is located on Disk #1 of the distribution discs. However, before you start the installation process you need to observe three important points.

1. Make sure your computer system has *at least* 1MB of RAM (random access memory) free for the use of the package. The minimum suitable combination is 640KB of 'conventional memory' and 384KB of 'extended memory'. If you bought your PC AT configured with 1MB of RAM, this will almost certainly be the combination. The more RAM your system has, the happier 1-2-3 will be, but it must have at least 384KB above the DOS partition configured as 'extended'. Above this, either extended or expanded memory will work equally well. If you intend to use 1-2-3 and Wysiwyg with the Auditor, Backsolver, Solver, and Viewer add-in programs, then you will need 3MB of RAM.

2. Your CONFIG.SYS file, in the root directory of the boot drive, must contain the following lines:

   Files=xx
   Buffers=yy

   Where xx and yy are numbers, at least equal to 20.

3. Your AUTOEXEC.BAT file, also in the root directory of the boot drive, must have a PATH statement which includes the directory in which you will place your 1-2-3 program files. The default for this is the directory 123R34, which you should keep, if at all possible. A typical PATH statement might be:

   PATH=C:\;C:\WINDOWS;C:\DOS;C:\123R34

   This would be suitable if your system boots up off the C: drive, your DOS files are placed in a directory called DOS, and both Microsoft Windows and 1-2-3 Release 3.4 are stored on the C: drive.

If you experience any problems while installing, starting or using 1-2-3, then refer to the information at the end of this chapter.

To install Release 3.4, first make sure that you have at least 7MB of free space on your hard disc (more if the available free space is fragmented), insert the 'Install' disc in the A: drive, type A: to log onto it, then type

   install

and press the <Enter> key.

Lotus 1-2-3 will display a screen in which you are asked to enter your name and your company's name. This information must be given when installing for the very first time with the distribution disc #1 (not a copy). When both these have been typed in, you must press the <Ins> key in order to proceed. Pressing the <Enter> key, simply moves the cursor to the next, or previous field. Subsequent installations of the program, cause 1-2-3 to retain the company name, but allows you to enter a different user's name. Having done so, do remember to press the <Ins> key in order to continue; pressing <Enter> has no effect. After verifying that the typed details are correct, you are presented with the 'Install' screen, shown on the next page.

4

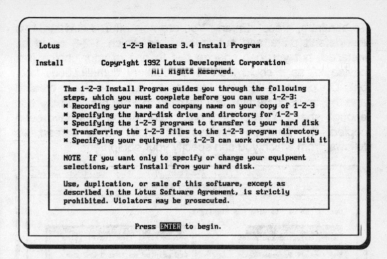

Pressing <Enter> causes the following display which informs you which files, corresponding to the listed programs, will be transferred on to your hard disc, if you continue.

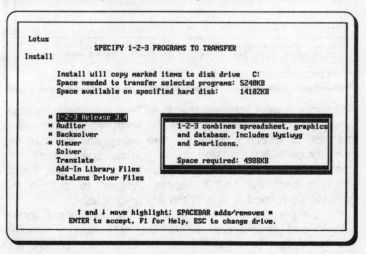

Lotus
                SPECIFY 1-2-3 PROGRAMS TO TRANSFER
Install

        Install will copy marked items to disk drive   C:
        Space needed to transfer selected programs: 5240KB
        Space available on specified hard disk: 14102KB

    ✳ 1-2-3 Release 3.4
    ✳ Auditor
    ✳ Backsolver   1-2-3 combines spreadsheet, graphics
    ✳ Viewer   and database. Includes Wysiwyg
      Solver   and SmartIcons.
      Translate
      Add-In Library Files   Space required: 4988KB
      DataLens Driver Files

        ↑ and ↓ move highlight; SPACEBAR adds/removes ✳
        ENTER to accept, F1 for Help, ESC to change drive.

To perform a complete installation, use the cursor keys to highlight, in turn, first the 'Solver', then the 'Translate', and following add-in programs, and pressing the <Space Bar> while each is highlighted, to add them to the installation list.

To continue, press <Enter>. You are now offered C:\123r34 as
the default drive and subdirectory on which 1-2-3 could be
installed, but you can change this to one of your choice (not
advisable, as it could lead to unecessary complications later
on). On pressing <Enter> the named subdirectory is created
and the appropriate files are transferred to it, provided there is
enough space on your hard disc. After all the files have been
copied, the program displays the 'Main Menu' screen, as
follows, from which you can specify your equipment.

```
                         M A I N   M E N U

   Use ↓ or ↑ to move the highlight.

   First-Time Installation        ┌──── First-Time Installation ────┐
   Change Selected Equipment      │ Select First-Time Installation  │
   Wysiwyg Options                │ to specify your screen display  │
   End Install Program            │ and printer so that 1-2-3 can   │
                                  │ work correctly with them. You   │
                                  │ must use First-Time Installation│
                                  │ before you can use 1-2-3.       │
                                  └─────────────────────────────────┘




   ↓ and ↑ move the highlight.        F1 displays a Help screen.
   ENTER selects highlighted choice.  F10 displays current selections.
```

From this screen, choose the 'First-Time Installation' option,
which provides you with step-by-step instructions for choosing
the type of screen adaptor you are using, and the text and
graphics printers you intend to use (you can specify more than
one printer). At a later stage, you can return to the 'Install'
program from the "1-2-3 Access System" to change the
selected equipment or specify the Wysiwyg options.

For the present, and after selecting the appropriate screen
adaptor and printers, proceed with the installation by selecting
the 'No' option from the 'Saving the Driver Set' screen, and
proceed with the installation of the fonts (for use with Wysiwyg),
by selecting the 'Medium' option. After some time, the program
displays the 'Installation Successful' screen, as shown on the
next page. On this screen, 'Help' reminds you what you have to
do to reconfigure your system so that you can run 1-2-3.

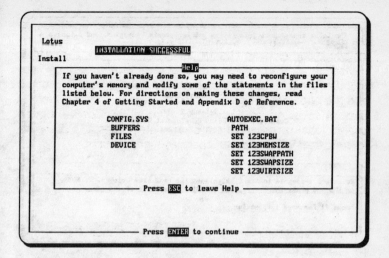

```
Lotus
Install     INSTALLATION SUCCESSFUL
                              Help
        If you haven't already done so, you may need to reconfigure your
        computer's memory and modify some of the statements in the files
        listed below. For directions on making these changes, read
        Chapter 4 of Getting Started and Appendix D of Reference.

                CONFIG.SYS                  AUTOEXEC.BAT
                 BUFFERS                     PATH
                 FILES                       SET 123CPBW
                 DEVICE                      SET 123MEMSIZE
                                             SET 123SWAPPATH
                                             SET 123SWAPSIZE
                                             SET 123VIRTSIZE

              ──── Press ESC to leave Help ────



              ──── Press ENTER to continue ────
```

Loading the 1-2-3 Program

If you are using a package which has already been installed on your computer's hard disc, then the 1-2-3 files should be found in a subdirectory, and the program can probably be invoked by typing **123** or **Lotus,** at the DOS prompt, provided the \123r34 subdirectory was included in the PATH command.

If, on the other hand, you have just installed the package yourself, in the suggested subdirectory, but you did not include this subdirectory in the PATH command, then a batch file will have to be written to locate the subdirectory in which the program's files reside and load the "1-2-3 Access System" into memory. To do this, use **edit** or a similar text editor to produce the following batch file (call it **lotus34.bat),** which could contain the following commands:

```
@echo off
cls
cd\ 123r34
lotus
cd\
```

If your system is correctly implemented, typing **lotus34** should cause the "1-2-3 Access Menu" to be displayed, as follows:

```
The Lotus spreadsheet integrating 3-D worksheets, graphics, and database
1-2-3        Install        Translate        Exit

                                Lotus
                           1-2-3 Access Menu

                              Release 3
               Copyright 1992 Lotus Development Corporation
                         All Rights Reserved.




To select a program to start, highlight the menu item using →, ←, HOME,
or END and press ENTER, or press the first character of the item.

Press F1 for more information.
```

The second line displays the Lotus menu which lists the options available to you. Note that option "1-2-3" is highlighted and that the highlighted bar can be moved by pressing the <Right> arrow, <Left> arrow or <Spacebar>.

Note also that as the highlighted bar moves, the description line above changes. This line explains what will happen if that particular option is selected. Selection of an option can also be made by typing its first character.

Loading the "1-2-3 Access Menu" takes time, and uses up some of your computer's memory because it remains resident. You can start 1-2-3 or any of its utilities, directly from the DOS prompt, by typing **123** (to load 1-2-3), **install** (to load Install), or **trans** (to load Translate) assuming you have added the \123r34 subdirectory to the PATH command as recommended, or by writing appropriate batch files.

Running 1-2-3:
To load 1-2-3, highlight the first option on the "1-2-3 Access Menu" and press <Enter>. This loads the appropriate program into your computer's memory, after first displaying the Lotus licence notice with a distinctive logo, together with details of the registered owner of the package. Once the program is loaded, a blank 2-dimensional worksheet appears on the screen, as with previous versions of 1-2-3. This is shown on the next page with Wysiwyg loaded, which is the default option.

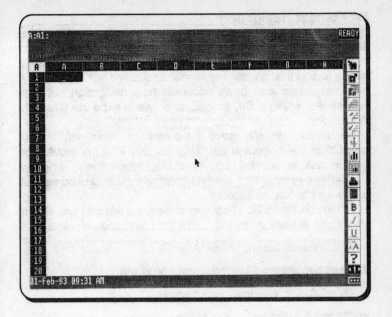

There are, however, some differences to a Lotus 1-2-3 version 2.x worksheet; the cell address in the top left hand corner of the screen reads:

A:A1:

The first A is the worksheet letter. As up to 256 sheets can be included in a file, 1-2-3 assigns a letter to each sheet opened. As with columns, individual sheets are labelled from A to IV. The worksheet letter can also be seen above the row numbers. The remainder of the cell reference gives, as before, the column and row 'co-ordinates'. Once you name the file in memory, the current filename replaces the clock indicator in the bottom left corner of the screen. If you have multiple files in memory this is often the only way of telling which file the cursor is actually in.

9

Worksheet Navigation

If you are not familiar with spreadsheets, we recommend you first work through the book "A Concise User's Guide to Lotus 1-2-3 Release 2.4". Those already familiar with 1-2-3, will be happy to find the familiar key combinations are still operative. A new range has also been added to help navigation between worksheets within a file, as well as between separate files held in memory.

The arrow keys still move the cursor up, down, left or right one cell in the current sheet. <PgUp> and <PgDn> moves the cursor one screen-full up, or down, respectively; whereas <Ctrl+Right Arrow> and <Ctrl+Left Arrow> move one screen-full to the right or left, as before.

To explain navigation between sheets, we will add two sheets to the one already in memory. Use the command sequences

/Worksheet, Insert, Sheet, After, 2

to insert two sheets after the current one, and

/Worksheet, Window, Perspective

to change the screen display to the following:

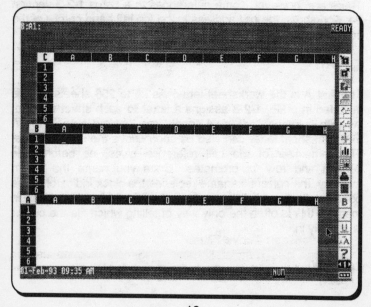

10

The same perspective can be displayed by placing the mouse pointer on the fourth SmartIcon and pressing the left mouse button.

Moving Between Sheets:
When multiple worksheets are displayed, the easiest way to move between them is with the mouse pointer. Clicking on a screen cell will make it the active cell. Clicking on the fifth SmartIcon of the first icon set, moves the active cell up one sheet, while clicking on the sixth SmartIcon moves the active cell down one sheet. The last SmartIcon at the bottom of the column of icons, marked with the '?' symbol will produce the help screen shown later.

With the keyboard, the <Ctrl+PgUp> and <Ctrl+PgDn> keys will move the cursor backwards and forwards between the active sheets. In other words with the cursor in sheet C pressing <Ctrl+PgDn> will move it to sheet B. These two key combinations work exactly the same way with multiple files in memory, as they move to the next active sheet, whether it is part of the current file or another one which is next in the 'stack'.

The <End Ctrl+PgUp> and <End Ctrl+PgDn> keys (press <End> followed by the other two keys together), move the cursor along the third dimension to the ends and beginnings of data blocks, (the equivalent to <End Arrow> in a 2-dimensional sheet) For example <End Ctrl+PgUp> will move through sheets, in ascending alphabetical order, to the next intersection of a blank and non-blank cell.

The <Ctrl+Home> key places the cursor in the first cell in the current file. From any sheet in the file it will return to cell A:A1. To get to the last cell in the current file you press <End Ctrl+Home>. The last cell in a file is the intersection of the last non-blank column, the last non-blank row and the last non-blank sheet.

These combinations may at first look a little complicated but they are a natural extension of those used previously on 2-dimensional sheets.

Moving Between Active Files:
There are four completely new movement commands for navigating between the files which are active, or open in memory.

<Ctrl+End Home> (**First File**) moves to the cell you last highlighted in the first file in the stack.

<Ctrl+End End> (**Last File**) moves to the cell you last highlighted in the last active file in memory.

<Ctrl+End Ctrl+PgUp> (**Next File**) moves to the last highlighted cell in the next active file.

<Ctrl+End Ctrl+PgDn> (**Prev File**) moves to the last highlighted cell in the previous active file in the stack.

The GOTO Key:
The GOTO key (**F5**) can still be used to move to any location on any sheet, or file, currently active. If you press **F5,** followed by **F3,** you get a list of all the named ranges in the current file, and all the other files in memory (which are enclosed in double-angled brackets). Using the mouse you can highlight these and move to any named location. Alternatively, from the **F5** prompt, you can type the cell reference and press <Enter>.

Using the Help System
Pressing **F1** or clicking the question mark SmartIcon, when in the READY mode, will produce the following screen:

12

You can move around the help index and bring up screens of information by clicking the mouse, or pressing <Enter>, on any highlighted topic. Any words shown on the screen in a contrasting colour represent related topics which also have help screens.

If you make a mistake in the program, 1-2-3 will beep and go into ERROR mode. Pressing HELP (**F1**) will give information of what went wrong, and suggest possible remedies.

Any time you are ready to leave HELP press <Esc> to return to the READY mode. For a description of 1-2-3 modes, see Appendix A.

The Undo Feature

A very useful feature Lotus have added to their most recent 1-2-3 packages is the ability to cancel some changes that have been made to a worksheet. This is done by pressing the UNDO key (Alt+**F4**). This feature will only function if it is first enabled with the

/Worksheet, Global, Default, Other, Undo, Enable

command. If you want to set this as the default do not forget to save the setting with the

/Worksheet, Global, Default, Update

command sequence.

When you press UNDO whilst in the READY mode 1-2-3 gives you the options either to do nothing, or to undo the most recent operations that have been carried out since the program was last in the READY mode.

The UNDO feature is not switched on when you use 1-2-3 for the first time. The main reason for this is that the facility creates a temporary back-up copy of all the data, and settings, affected by the current operation. This uses computer memory that may otherwise be needed to run the program. Unless your computer is fitted with a large amount of RAM, you may find you have to disable UNDO frequently, especially if you work with large macros or spreadsheets.

To see some more information on the UNDO feature, click on the '?' SmartIcon with the left mouse button (or press **F1**) to display the 'Help' screen, and select the 'Undo Feature' from the list of help items. The following text appears on your screen:

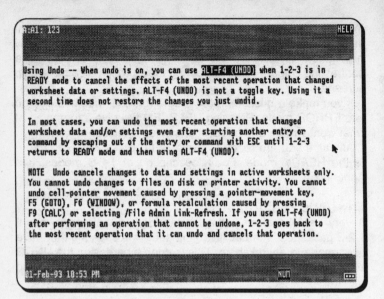

Using Undo -- When undo is on, you can use ALT-F4 (UNDO) when 1-2-3 is in
READY mode to cancel the effects of the most recent operation that changed
worksheet data or settings. ALT-F4 (UNDO) is not a toggle key. Using it a
second time does not restore the changes you just undid.

In most cases, you can undo the most recent operation that changed
worksheet data and/or settings even after starting another entry or
command by escaping out of the entry or command with ESC until 1-2-3
returns to READY mode and then using ALT-F4 (UNDO).

NOTE Undo cancels changes to data and settings in active worksheets only.
You cannot undo changes to files on disk or printer activity. You cannot
undo cell-pointer movement caused by pressing a pointer-movement key,
F5 (GOTO), F6 (WINDOW), or formula recalculation caused by pressing
F9 (CALC) or selecting /File Admin Link-Refresh. If you use ALT-F4 (UNDO)
after performing an operation that cannot be undone, 1-2-3 goes back to
the most recent operation that it can undo and cancels that operation.

01-Feb-93 10:53 PM   NUM

Using Function Keys

Each function key, with the exception of **F5**, performs two
operations; one when pressed by itself, and another when
pressed with the **Alt** key held down.

All the 1-2-3 function keys, together with their names, and
details of what they do when pressed, are listed in the table
below.

Key	Name	Description
F1	HELP	Displays a 1-2-3 Help screen.
F2	EDIT	Enters EDIT mode and displays the current cell contents in the control panel.
F3	NAME	Displays a menu of range names. When entering a formula, pressing **F3** after an arithmetic operator or a parenthesis, displays a list of range names which can then be included in the formula.
F4	ABS	Switches a cell, or a range of cells, between relative, absolute, and mixed addressing.

14

F5	GOTO	Moves the cell pointer to a specified location, or active file.
F6	WINDOW	Moves the cell pointer between windows created with the **/Worksheet, Window** command.
F7	QUERY	Repeats the most recent **/Data, Query** operation.
F8	TABLE	Repeats most recent **/Data, Table** operation.
F9	CALC	Recalculates all formulae (READY mode). Converts a formula to its value (VALUE and EDIT modes).
F10	GRAPH	Displays the current graph, or creates an automatic graph using the data around the cell pointer.
Alt+F1	COMPOSE	When used with alphanumeric keys, creates characters you can't enter directly from the keyboard.
Alt+F2	RECORD	Enables the contents of the record buffer, or turns on the STEP mode, which executes macros one step at a time to facilitate debugging.
Alt+F3	RUN	Displays a menu of named worksheet ranges so that you can select the name of a macro to run.
Alt+F4	UNDO	When enabled, it cancels changes made to the worksheet since 1-2-3 was last in READY mode.
Alt+F6	ZOOM	Switches the current window between reduced and full-screen sizes.
Alt+F7	APP1	Activates add-in program assigned to key, if any.
Alt+F8	APP2	Similar to APP1.
Alt+F9	APP3	Similar to APP1.
Alt+F10	ADDIN	Displays a 1-2-3 add-in menu.
Ctrl+F9	DISPLAY ICONS	With Wysiwyg & in READY mode, it hides or displays the icon palette.
Ctrl+F10	SELECT ICONS	With Wysiwyg & in READY mode, it allows icon selection with arrow keys.

The README.PRN File

Lotus has included a file called README.WK3 which can be retrieved in the usual way by issuing the /**File, Retrieve** command. Doing so, reveals the following screen:

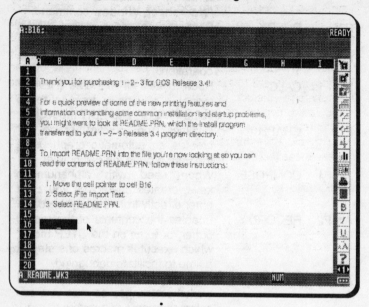

In this screen you are told how to import a text file which gives you information on the following items:

- Suggested solutions on problems you might encounter while installing, starting or using 1-2-3.

- Explanation on how to use the utility 'BPrint' to change to background printing.

- Useful information to upgraders.

If you have any problems while installing or starting 1-2-3, then use instead the

    Edit \123r34\README.PRN

command to read the file with the use of the DOS editor.

2. THREE-DIMENSIONAL SHEETS

In 1-2-3 a 3-dimensional file is one made up with a series of flat 2-dimensional worksheets stacked 'on top of each other'. Each sheet is the same size, and in itself, behaves the same as the more ordinary worksheets of previous 1-2-3 versions. As mentioned in the previous chapter, each separate sheet in a file has its own identification letter in its top left-hand corner. Ranges can be set to span several different sheets to build up 3-dimensional blocks of data. These blocks can then be manipulated, copied, or moved to other locations in the file. A cell can reference any other cell in the file, no matter what sheet it is on, and an extended range of functions can be used to process these 3-dimensional ranges.

Manipulating Ranges

The best way to demonstrate a new idea is to work through an example. We will start with a very simplistic one. If you do not have 1-2-3 running on your computer load it into memory and start with an empty sheet. Insert another two blank sheets using the

> /Worksheet, Insert, Sheet, After, 2

command, as described previously, then select the

> /Worksheet, Window, Perspective

command so that you can see, and work with, a part of each sheet. Press <Ctrl+Home> to move the cursor to cell A:A1, the top of the file, and type **JANUARY**. Then enter **Week 1** in cell A:A2 and **Week 2** in cell A:B2.

To copy between sheets place the cursor on cell A:A2 and use the command sequence

> /Copy, <-→>, <Enter>

to select the range to copy from as A:A2..A:B2. Then press <Ctrl+PgUp>, to move the cursor to cell B:A2 on the next sheet, type a period (.) to anchor the cell pointer and press <Ctrl+PgUp> to select the range B:A2..C:B2 as the destination.

Your screen should now look like the one below:

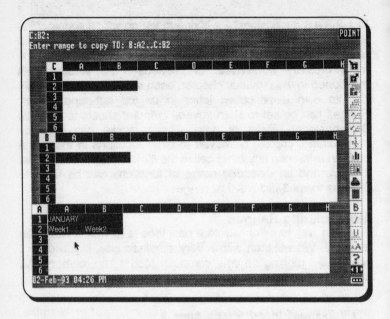

Pressing <Enter> will cause the copy operation to take place.

Next, type **FEBRUARY** and **MARCH** in cells B:A1 and C:A1, respectively. You now have the start of what could be a 3-dimensional matrix which could be used to store data, such as sales or costs, with a different sheet allocated for each month.

To demonstrate a 3-dimensional range place the cursor in cell A:A1 and invoke the

/Range, Name, Create

command, type **Months** as the name, and press <Enter>. Now press the <↓> and <→> arrows to highlight the range A:A1..A:B2 and then press <Ctrl+PgUp> twice. The range A:A1..C:B2 is now highlighted as shown on the next page.

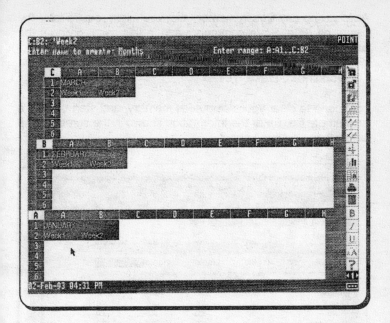

Pressing <Enter> will accept the range. If you wanted you could move this range to another location in the file. For example, with the cursor in cell A:F4 activate the /**Move** command, type **Months** as the range to move from, and press <Enter> to accept A:F4 as the location to move to. The whole range should now have moved to the cells A:F4..C:G5.

Spreadsheet Design

There is probably very little that you can now do with 1-2-3's 3-dimensional ability that would not have been possible, albeit with some ingenuity, in previous versions of the program. The overall efficiency however has been enormously improved.

Parallel Sheet Layouts:

Similar data can now be put in parallel, identically formatted, sheets, each one of which applies to, for example, a different period of time. As a demonstration of this approach to spreadsheet layout, we will build up a file of sheets to analyse the trading figures of a small consulting company.

19

After saving any files in memory that you might require later (by using the /**File, Save** command, and in this case, giving it the name **Months**), use the

/**Worksheet, Erase, Yes**

command to clear your computer's memory, and start off with a new empty file. Enter the information shown in the screen dump below in the empty A sheet.

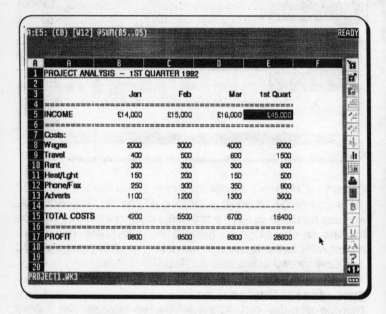

In the example shown, the cell widths of columns A-F have been set at 12. To do this, place the cursor in the home cell (A:A1), use the command sequence

/**Worksheet, Column, Column-Range, Set-Width**

select the range A1..F1, then type **12** followed by <Enter>.

With Release 3.4, provided Wysiwyg is invoked, certain enhancements can be made to your worksheet. The title label, in cell A1, is shown both bold and underlined.

20

To do this, place the cursor in the A1 cell and select the Wysiwyg menu by right clicking the mouse when the pointer is in the menu zone, or by pressing the colon (:) key. Thus, select

   :Format, Bold, Set

followed by

   :Format, Underline, Single

to carry out emboldening and underlining, respectively. Similarly all the sheet titles in row 3 and column A could be emboldened.

Note: A look through the Wysiwyg menus during the above operations shows that you can change the fonts and colour of characters, select bold and italics, carry out several types of underlining and place both lines and shading on a worksheet. All these enhancements show immediately on the screen and carry through to the final printed product.

The '1st Quarter' income, in cell E5, is calculated with the function

   @SUM(B5..D5)

This function (see Appendix B for all 1-2-3 functions) can be copied to the range E8..E13. Similarly the 'Total Costs' shown for January in cell B15 are the sum of the range B8..B13.

Any range of rows or columns can be added up by simply highlighting the range (see next section on how to do this) and including one empty cell (on the right of the range for summing rows, or at the bottom of the range for summing columns), and then pointing and clicking the left mouse button at the '1+2=3' SmartIcon (the 7th on palete 1). To select this icon with the keyboard, press Ctrl+**F10**, use the ↑ & ↓ arrow keys to highlight the icon and press <Enter>.

The 'Profit', in B17, is the difference between 'Income' and 'Costs', calculated by the formula

   +B5-B15

To complete the entry, both the @SUM( ) relationship and the above formula should be copied into the three cells to their right.

To make sure you do not lose your work, save the file to disk using the **/File, Save** command and typing the name PROJECT1. Note that as soon as you have carried out this operation the file name replaces the time/date information previously displayed on the bottom screen line. Your screen should now look the same as that shown previously.

Working with SmartIcons

Over 80 SmartIcons, organised in 8 palettes, are provided in Release 3.4; a palette being a column of icons that appears on the extreme right-hand side of the 1-2-3 display. Which palette is currently displayed is indicated by the number that appears at the bottom of the column of icons. Each palette also holds the '?' (Help) SmartIcon, which appears as the last icon in each set.

The first palette (identified by the <1> at the very bottom of the icons) can be customised to display the icons you most frequently use. The icons in the remaining palettes are fixed; you can copy them to the first palette, but you cannot move them or delete them. The last palette of icons (identified by U1 through to U12) are user icons to which you can assign macros.

To activate a SmartIcon use the mouse to point to it and click the left mouse button (or press Ctrl+**F10** and use the ↑ & ↓ arrow keys to select it, then press <Enter>).

Selecting a Range:

In most cases, you are required to select a range of cells before activating a SmartIcon, which can be done with either the mouse or the keyboard. With the mouse, drag the cell pointer (by pressing the left mouse button and keeping it pressed while moving the mouse) to highlight the required range. With the keyboard, move the cell pointer to the first cell of the range, press either **F4** or a full stop (.) to anchor the cursor, use the arrow keys to highlight the required range, and press <Enter>.

To change palettes with the mouse, point to one of the arrows on either side of the palette number and click the left mouse button to scroll forward or backward through the various palettes. With the keyboard, first press Ctrl+**F10** to select the first icon of the current palette, then press the → arrow to scroll forward or the ← arrow to scroll backward.

To hide or display a palette, either click the icon with the three small squares (under the palette number), or press Ctrl+**F9**.

To find out what each SmartIcon does, point to the required icon with the mouse pointer and hold down the right mouse button. A brief message appears at the top of the screen, describing the function of the chosen icon. With the keyboard, this message is displayed when the icon is selected.

Working with Palettes:
The custom palette, palette 1, is the only one that you can customise. It should display the icons you use most often. SmartIcons can be added to, removed from or rearranged within the custom palette, with the use of three special SmartIcons which are to be found in palette 7. These icons are shown below as they display in the Wysiwyg mode. A complete list of all SmartIcons is to be found in Appendix C.

Icon	*Function*
	The ***Add icon*** allows you to add a selected icon to your custom palette. You can select any icon from any other palette, which 1-2-3 then copies to the last position in the custom palette. If the custom palette is full, the last icon in it is replaced by the selected icon.
	The ***Del icon*** allows you to delete a selected icon from your custom palette. When you select this icon, 1-2-3 displays the custom palette so that you can remove unwanted icons. Having done so, you can then add new icons.
	The ***Move icon*** allows you to rearrange the icons in your custom palette. When you select this icon, 1-2-3 displays the custom palette and waits for you to select the icon you want to move, and indicate the position to which you want to move it. Moving an icon above or below its present position, forces all the icons below or above it to move down or up one position, respectively.

Customising the User Icons:
If you have a unique set of tasks which are often repeated, and 1-2-3 hasn't a SmartIcon to do the job, then it is easy to set one of the 'user icons' to achieve your requirements. To do this, select the *User icon* (the last icon from palette 7 - which looks as follows and has the following function:

Icon   *Function*

                   The **User icon** allows you to write a set of instructions to carry out a given process, and attach it to one of the 'user icons' (to be found in palette 7).

Let us assume we would like to attach to the U1 user icon the

   /Range, Erase

command.
   On activating the *User icon*, 1-2-3 displays the following dialogue box on your screen:

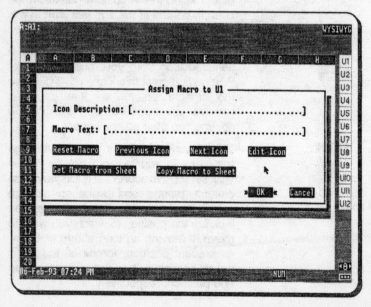

The dialogue box heading indicates which user icon is selected, (U1 in this case). Select 'Icon Description' field and enter the namo *Erase Range*. Then select the 'Macro Text' field and type

    /RE

and click on the **OK** button (or press <Enter>). To use the icon, highlight a range of worksheet cells and activate icon U1.

You can even edit the icon you have assigned your macro to, by selecting 'Edit Icon' from the above 'Assign Macro' dialogue box. If you select 'Edit Icon', the U1 icon is presented on screen magnified and ready for you to change it.

Group Mode:
Once you have completed the worksheet entries for the 1st Quarter's trading results you will need to insert another sheet, into the file, on which to build the 2nd Quarter's figures.

To simplify this operation, 1-2-3 now has a 'GROUP' mode facility which groups all the sheets in a file together. When used, this assigns the cell settings and formats of the current sheet (that in which the cursor is currently placed) to any other sheets in the file. This makes it very easy to prepare a series of identical parallel sheets in a file. GROUP mode also affects the action of the cursor when moving between the sheets of a file. When set, it keeps the pointer in the same cell in each worksheet as you move between sheets. When not set the pointer highlights the last cell that was active when the sheet was last used.

In our example the second sheet needs the same settings as the first, so use the

   /Worksheet, Global, Group, Enable

command to switch the facility on. Whenever GROUP mode is selected, a status indicator is displayed on the bottom screen line. Insert a second sheet (B), behind the present one, with the

   /Worksheet, Insert, Sheet, After

command. The contents of this second parallel sheet should be as follows:

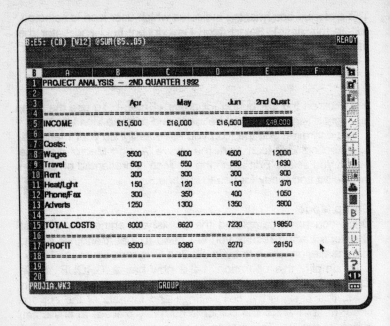

B	A	B	C	D	E	F
1	PROJECT ANALYSIS — 2ND QUARTER 1992					
2						
3		Apr	May	Jun	2nd Quart	
4	=====	=====	=====	=====	=====	
5	INCOME	£15,500	£16,000	£16,500	£48,000	
6	=====	=====	=====	=====	=====	
7	Costs:					
8	Wages	3500	4000	4500	12000	
9	Travel	500	550	580	1630	
10	Rent	300	300	300	900	
11	Heat/Lght	150	120	100	370	
12	Phone/Fax	300	350	400	1050	
13	Adverts	1250	1300	1350	3900	
14						
15	TOTAL COSTS	6000	6620	7230	19850	
16	=====	=====	=====	=====	=====	
17	PROFIT	9500	9380	9270	28150	
18	=====	=====	=====	=====	=====	
19						
20						

PROJ1A.WK3   GROUP

The easiest way to enter these 2nd Quarter results is to copy the original data from sheet A and then edit it using the EDIT key (**F2**). This way all the formats and formulae will not need duplicating. Place the cursor in cell A:A1, choose /**Copy,** press the <End Home> <Enter> keys to select all the sheet data as the range to copy from, and press <Ctrl+PgUp> <Enter> to select B:A1 as the location to copy to.

You should now be in a position to complete editing sheet B. Be extra careful, from now on, to check the identification letter in the top left corner of each worksheet, as it is easy to get the sheets mixed up. You do not want to spend time editing the wrong worksheet!

After building up the four worksheets (one for each quarter) save the file as PROJECT2.

Linking Worksheets

A consolidation sheet could be placed in front of our 'stack' of data sheets to show a full year's results, as follows:

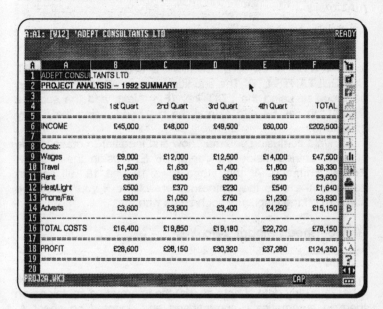

The blank sheet for this was inserted with the pointer in the previous sheet A and with the GROUP mode still active. Note that as it was inserted in front, 1-2-3 labelled it as the A sheet and relabelled the other worksheets. To avoid confusion, it pays to plan your layout before you start inserting any worksheets, otherwise it is very easy to find you have built up a 3-dimensional file which is completely 'back to front'.

Editing a Worksheet:

As before, the easiest way to complete this worksheet is to copy all the data from sheet B onto sheet A and edit the result. You will need to turn the GROUP mode off using the

   /Worksheet, Global, Group, Disable

command, so that the editing process will be independent of the other sheets in the file, otherwise any changes you make will be reflected in all the other sheets.

27

As the consolidation sheet is at the front of the file it should contain the main title. In our case we will place this in the home cell, so we must first make room for it. With the pointer in cell A:A1 press

/Worksheet, Insert, Row

to insert a blank row as a new row1, and enter the title ADEPT CONSULTANTS LTD. The sub-titles in cells A2 and B4..E4 can be modified using the EDIT key (F2). Next, add the sub-title 'TOTAL' in cell F4 and extend the five lines, using the /Copy command.

To avoid confusion you may now find it easier to erase all the numeric entries inside the range B6..E14 using the /Range, Erase command. At this stage rows 16 and 18 will contain zeros as the cells they reference are blank. If you prefer you can turn off the display of such zeros with the

/Worksheet, Global, Zero, Yes

command.

You are now in a position to link the consolidation sheet to the other quarterly data sheets so that the information contained on them is automatically summarised and updated on sheet A. This operation is much easier to carry out when you can see several sheets at the same time. Use the

/Worksheet, Window, Perspective

command to show the top few lines of sheets A, B and C together. Place the pointer in cell A:B6 and enter the formula

+B:E5

The contents of the cell B:E5, the 'Total Income for the 1st Quarter', are now also placed in cell A:B6. This is a dynamic linkage, if the contents of the cell on the data sheet are changed, the change will also be reflected on the consolidation sheet. In the same way, link the totals for the other quarters to their respective data sheets. Move the pointer to the 'Total Income' cell F6 and enter the function

@SUM(B6..E6)

If necessary use the command

/Range, Format, Currency, 0

to format the cell correctly. Your screen display should now look
similar to that below:

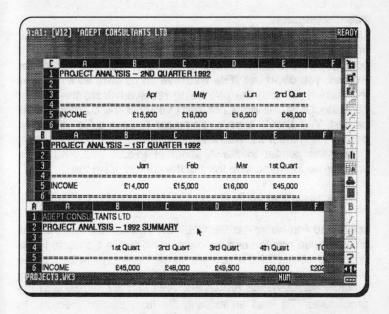

To finish the entries in the consolidation worksheet you will
need a full screen display of the data. Press the ZOOM key
(Alt+**F6**) to achieve this. This key toggles the display between
perspective and full screen views when the perspective view is
activated.

All that now remains to complete the consolidation sheet
entries can be done in one operation. Copy the contents of the
range A:B6..A:F6 to the 'Costs' area range A:B9..A:F14. Your
resultant display should look the same as the screen dump of
the consolidation sheet, shown in 'Linking Worksheets' section.

As you may want to use this file in later examples we suggest
you save it as PROJECT3.

Linking Files

In the last example we built a consolidation report on a separate worksheet in front of several parallel data sheets. All these sheets were, however, part of the same file. There may be times, possibly for security purposes, when the consolidation data would be preferable in a completely separate file. As an example of linking files together we will work through an exercise to carry out this operation.

File Commands:

Use the /**Worksheet, Erase, Yes** command to clear your memory, and /**File, Retrieve** to load the file PROJECT2.WK3. If you only had one file active in memory, that you no longer wanted, you could use /**File Retrieve** on its own, as it replaces the current file with the one being retrieved. **Note** the danger here though, 1-2-3 does not warn you that the current file will be lost. You should always remember to save a file you need, before using the /**File, Retrieve** command.

With the pointer in the A sheet of PROJECT2.WK3 place another file in memory, in front of the cursor, using the

/**File, New, Before**

command and name the file ADEPT1. You can tell that the new file has been created and is now current, by the file name in the left hand corner of the screen. Move between the two active files in memory, using either the mouse pointer or the key commands discussed previously, until you are happy with the procedures. To load an existing file from disk to memory, to make it active, you would use the /**File, Open** command.

As with the previous example, the easiest way to complete the consolidation file is to copy all the data from sheet A of the file PROJECT2.WK3 onto sheet A of ADEPT1.WK3 and edit the result. Copying between files is the same as copying between the separate sheets of a file. Do not try to 'move' data between files, however, as this is not allowed. Place the pointer in cell A:A1 of file PROJECT2.WK3, use the /**Copy** command, select all of the data as the range to copy from, then press <Ctrl+PgDn> to move the pointer to the other file. Press the down arrow so that the pointer is in cell A:A2 and look at the range name shown in the second screen line.

Your path may be different, but in our case it is:

....range to copy TO: <<A:\123r3\ADEPT1.WK3>>A:A2

Cell references between different files are shown with the path and file name, included in double angular brackets (<<...>>), placed before the cell address. The easiest way to enter such references is to highlight the required cell when in POINT mode, as described above. You can also type them if you prefer.

To complete the exercise, edit the consolidation sheet as in the previous example. The screen dump below shows how the linkage between the sheets is effected. With the pointer in the '2nd Quarter Income' cell, <<..\ADEPT1.WK3>>A:C6, type + and POINT the cursor to cell <<..\PROJECT2.WK3>>B:E5.

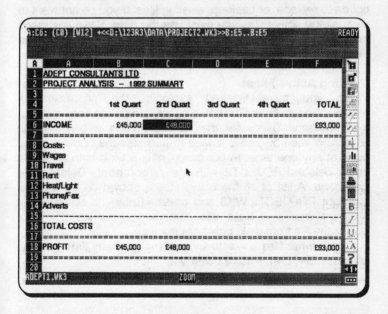

Pressing <Enter> completes the linkage. When you have finished editing the worksheet it should look similar to that shown on page 18, but with the file name ADEPT1.WK3.

Refreshing Linkages:
Whenever a file that is linked to another is retrieved into memory, with the **/File, Open** or **/File, Retrieve** commands, the formulae that contain the linkages must be 'updated' by using

  /File, Admin, Link-Refresh

This command recalculates formulae in active files that include references to other active files, or to files on disk. Unfortunately this is NOT automatically carried out by 1-2-3.

Saving Multiple Files:
When more than one file is active you can save them all at the same time with the **/File, Save** command. The program, in this case, defaults to [ALL MODIFIED FILES] and then gives the option to replace, or back-up, existing files. If you do not want to save all the active files you must use the **/File, Save** command from each file that you want to save, press <Esc> to remove the default prompt and then press <Enter> to save that file.

Deleting Active Files:
When you have finished exploring the processes of manipulating multiple files you may want to delete one, or more, from memory. Every file that is active uses a considerable amount of memory, so it is wise to minimise the number being used at any one time. In our case, after saving both files, you could delete PROJECT2 with the **/Worksheet, Delete, File** command. A list of all the active files is shown on the screen, highlight PROJECT2.WK3 and press <Enter> to remove that file from memory. **Note** this command sequence does not delete the file from disk, only from memory.

  To see what files are actually in memory at any time you can use the **/File, List, Active** command.

3. USING THE PRINT COMMANDS

You might have discovered by now that it is possible to print a worksheet either from within 1-2-3 with the **/Print, Printer** command, or from within Wysiwyg with the **:Print** command.

The /Print Command

Users of older versions of 1-2-3 will immediately notice that many additions have been made to the **/Print** command menus. This command now produces an extra sub-menu:

Printer File Encoded Background Suspend Resume Cancel

The first three options control the print destination. **Printer** sends output to the current printer, **File** produces an ASCII text file on disk and **Encoded** produces a print file on disk, with all the printer control codes embedded in it. Such files can be used on any suitable printer, without needing the 1-2-3 program, by entering a DOS command, such as:

COPY *Filename.Ext* LPT1

Background sends your print output to a temporary encoded file, the name and path of which you specify, and then prints in the background, allowing you to carry on with other spreadsheet work. For this procedure to operate, you must first activate the background printing program by typing **BPRINT** at the DOS prompt before you run 1-2-3. To automate this procedure, you could add the command **BPRINT** to the start up file **lotus34.bat** described under section 'Loading the 1-2-3 Program' in Chapter 1. Make sure you place this line between the 'cd\ 123r34' and the 'lotus' commands in the file.

The other options on the first menu line are needed to control the background printing. **Suspend** and **Resume** are used to stop and start background printing, whereas **Cancel** ends the operation.

Printer Set Up:

When 1-2-3 was first installed on your computer the printer, or printers, to be used should have been selected and their 'drivers' made available to the program. To see if this has been carried out correctly, use the

/Print, Printer, Options

command, which produces the dialogue box shown below.

```
Range  Line  Page  Options  Clear  Align  Go  Image  Hold  Quit
Header  Footer  Margins  Borders  Setup  Pg-Length  Other  Name  Advanced  Quit
                              Print Settings
 ┌─Print──────────────────────────────────────────────────────────────────┐
 │ Printer x    Text file        Encoded file        Background           │
 │ File name:                                                              │
 │ Printer Name: Apple LaserWriter Plus Times/Helvetica                    │
 │ Interface:    Parallel 1                                                │
 └────────────────────────────────────────────────────────────────────────┘
   Range:
 ┌─Options────────────────────────────────────────────────────────────────┐
 │ Header:                                                                 │
 │ Footer:                                                                 │
 │ Margins:    Left: 4        Right: 76      Top: 2        Bottom: 2       │
 │ Borders:                                                                │
 │   Columns:              Rows:                     No Frame              │
 │ Setup string:                                                           │
 │ Page length: 66                                                         │
 │ Other:     Print Range(s):  Formatted      As-Displayed                │
 │            Blank Headers and Footers: Printed                           │
 └────────────────────────────────────────────────────────────────────────┘
   Image:
```

Should it be necessary to change your printer selection, use the command sequence

/Print, Printer, Options, Advanced, Device, Name

This should produce a list of numbers with each one referring to an installed printer. Select the number for the printer you require, or, if it is not listed, exit 1-2-3 and run the Install program as described in the first chapter. Once you have selected your printer you can select the settings you require from the 'Print Settings' dialogue box shown above.

You will probably only need to use the other commands in the **/Print** menu if you want to print your worksheets without the Wysiwyg module being attached. In this book we assume that you will be using the Wysiwyg module, so we will not pursue these other commands any further.

The Wysiwyg :Print Command

To check the effect of your printer settings, and obtain some practice in using the SmartIcons, use the procedure detailed on the next page. Note that in what follows we only refer to SmartIcons in the permanent palettes (other than palette 1). This is done intentionally, because it is quite possible that you have experimented with the icons in palette 1 and have perhaps changed the order in which they appeared when you first installed the package.

- Retrieve PROJECT3, activate the 'Window Perspective' SmartIcon (the 2nd of palette 5), to clear the Window Perspective and display worksheet A in full screen.

- Select range A4..E6 by highlighting it, and activate the 'Graph' SmartIcon (the 9th of palette 6), and press the <OK> button on the displayed dialogue box to see the graph of 'Income' in a 3-D bar chart.

- Press <Esc> to return to the worksheet, then select range B9..E119 by highlighting it, then activate the 'Graph on Worksheet' SmartIcon (the 10th of palette 6).

- Select range A1..F20 by highlighting it, then activate the 'Preview' SmartIcon (the 6th of palette 6).

If you make any mistakes, use the /**File, Retrieve** command to reload PROJECT3 into memory, and start again. Once you are satisfied that all is as it should be, save the resultant worksheet as ADEPT2. Finally, to print your work on paper,

- Select range A1..F20 by highlighting it, then activate the 'Print' SmartIcon (the 5th of palette 6).

As mentioned previously, it is possible to print either from within 1-2-3 with the /**Print, Printer** command or from within Wysiwyg with the :**Print** command.

Here, because we are using the 'Printer' SmartIcon, we are effectively printing from within Wysiwyg (as SmartIcons will not be displayed unless Wysiwyg is attached). There is a subtle difference between the two printing methods, which will be explained later.

If your printer is properly installed, the output from it should be as shown below:

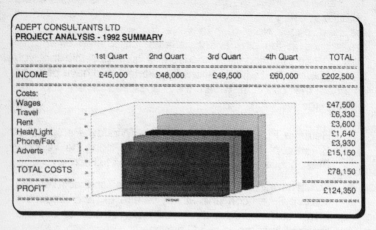

ADEPT CONSULTANTS LTD
PROJECT ANALYSIS - 1992 SUMMARY

	1st Quart	2nd Quart	3rd Quart	4th Quart	TOTAL
INCOME	£45,000	£48,000	£49,500	£60,000	£202,500
Costs:					
Wages					£47,500
Travel					£6,330
Rent					£3,600
Heat/Light					£1,640
Phone/Fax					£3,930
Adverts					£15,150
TOTAL COSTS					£78,150
PROFIT					£124,350

The Wysiwyg Print Settings Sheet:

When you select the **:Print** command, a 'Settings Sheet' is opened, as shown below:

```
A:A1:                                                          WYSIWYG
Go  File  Background  Range  Config  Settings  Layout  Preview  Info  Quit
Print the specified range

  Print range(s)....                    Margins (in inches)

  Layout:                                    Top 0.5
    Paper type... A4
    Page size.... 8.268 by 11.693 inches
    Titles:                             Left          Right
      Header.....                       0.5           0.5
      Footer.....
    Top border...
    Left border..                       Bottom 0.55
    Compression.. None
                                        Settings:
  Configuration:                          Begin......... 1
    Printer...... Apple LaserWriter Plus Ti...   End............ 9999
    Interface.... Parallel 1              Start-Number.. 1
    Cartridges...                         Copies........ 1
    Orientation.. Portrait                Wait.......... No
    Resolution... Final                   Grid.......... No
    Bin..........                         Frame......... No

09-Feb-93 05:55 PM
```

Any changes to this sheet must be made before the print destination is selected (**Go** to send output to the printer and **File** to send output to a print file on disc).

Most of the time, the **Range Set** and **Go** commands are all you will need to print most worksheets. If, however, you would like to control the way your printout will look on the page, then you will need to use the three sub-menu options of the **Layout** command. These are **Page-Size**, **Margins**, and **Titles**.

If you are using cut-sheet paper in the U.K., select A4 for page size. The **Margins** option lets you set the top, bottom, left and right margins. The default values for these is 0.5 inches for the top, left and right margins, and 0.55 inches for the bottom margin. All four margins can be reduced to 0, but some printers, such as the Hewlett-Packard LaserJet and DeskJet 500, require top and bottom margins of at least 0.5 inches if they are to function correctly. Finally, the **Titles** option sets your printout's headers and footers which are normally left-aligned within the print range. To centre such titles, precede the text with a split vertical line (|), and to right-align them, precede the text with two split vertical lines (||).

It is a good idea to check the effect of your choices in the Print Settings dialogue box by using the **Preview** command. A very useful feature included in Release 3.4 is the **Compression** option on the **Layout** menu. If you set this to **Automatic**, Wysiwyg will adjust the size of your print output so that the whole of the selected range will fit across the width of your page. Obviously, if your worksheet range is very wide, this will produce text so small that you will not be able to read it. Used carefully, it does mean that you can produce print output to fit your page without manually adjusting the fonts or the width of your sheet columns.

Printing in Landscape Mode:

Lotus 1-2-3, Release 3.4 also allows you to print to a laser or dot-matrix printer in *landscape mode* which prints along the length of the paper. This is imperative if your spreadsheet is wider than the paper you are printing on. The mode, 'Portrait' or 'Landscape' can be selected by using the Wysiwyg command

:Print, Config, Orientation

Printing to an Encapsulated PostScript File:
The program also includes a driver that allows you to print to an *encapsulated PostScript file* (an .EPS file) which can contain both text and graphics. Such a file can then be used by other programs, such as a word processing or a desktop publishing program.

However, before you can print to an .EPS file, you must install the encapsulated PostScript file driver. If you have not done so already, use the 'Install' option from the Lotus 1-2-3 Access menu and select the 'Change Selected Equipment' option from the Main menu. Now, choose 'Modify the Current DCF', then 'Change Selected Printer' and select 'PostScript' from the list of printers, and choose 'PostScript EPSF' from the three options displayed. Finally, return to the previous menu and select 'Save Changes' and accept the default drive/path and filename by pressing <Enter>. Then follow the instructions relating to which disc number to insert to the A: drive so that the appropriate printer driver can be transferred to your hard disc.

You can check that the encapsulated PostScript file driver is safely installed by using the Wysiwyg

:Print, Config, Printer

command which should then list the required driver, together with the other print drivers you have specified in a dialogue box.

4. SPREADSHEET GRAPHS

Lotus 1-2-3 allows Information within a workshoot to be represented in graphical form which makes data more accessible to non-expert users who might not be familiar with the spreadsheet format. The package allows the use of several chart and graph types, including line, bar, stacked bar, pie, and mixed charts.

Types of Charts

On selecting the **/Graph** command, the 'Graph Settings' dialogue box is displayed as follows:

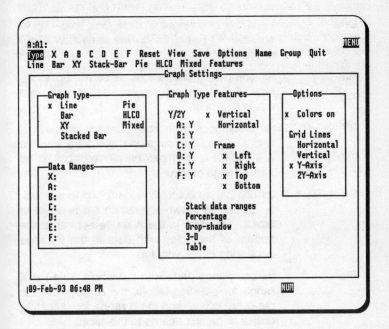

Within the 'Graph Type' option, you have the following choice of charts:

Line Bar XY Stack-Bar Pie HLCO Mixed Features

Once you have chosen a chart type, you can add titles, legends, labels, and can select grids, scaling, fonts, etc. These charts (you can have several per spreadsheet) can be displayed on the screen and can be sent to an appropriate output device, such as a plotter or printer. As long as the Wysiwyg add-in is active, you can also superimpose your chart on the worksheet and see changes made to the worksheet reflected immediately on the redrawn chart.

On selecting one of the options under 'Type', 1-2-3 expects you to define the X data range, followed by up to six (A - F) y-axis data ranges. The seven main graph-types are normally used when we would like to describe the following relationships between data:

Line	for showing changes in data over time - up to six sets, A - F, can be drawn against an x-axis range of labels.
Bar	for comparing differences in data - up to six sets, A - F, can be drawn against an x-axis range of labels.
XY	for showing scatter relationships between X and Y - up to six points on the chart (using the A - F data range) can be plotted against an x-axis range of values.
Stack-Bar	for comparing cumulative data - up to six sets, A - F, can be drawn against an x-axis range of labels. The data in the A range appear at the bottom of the stack with data in the F range appearing at the very top.
Pie	for comparing parts with the whole. Use the X range for pie-slice labels, the A range for the pie-slice values, and the B range for allocating colour or hatch patterns to the slices.
HLCO	for showing the extreme high and low fluctuations of data values with time, together with their corresponding closing and opening values during that period. The X data range is used to specify the x-axis labels, with ranges A, B, C and D being used for the sets of high,

low, close, and open values, respectively. The E range can be used as a set of bars below the HLCO area, while the F range can be used as a line in the HLCO area. This type of chart is useful for describing opening and closing trading figures of shares in the stock market.

Mixed   for showing different types of data on the same graph; they are combinations of bar and line graphs. The X data range is used for the x-axis labels, while ranges A, B, and C are used as sets of bars, and ranges D, E, and F are used as sets of lines.

The **Features** option of the **/Graph, Type** command, offers the following ten charting capabilities:

Vertical   Displays a horizontal x-axis across the bottom of the graph, with a vertical y-axis along the left edge of the graph. This is the default choice.

Horizontal   Displays the chart rotated by 90 degrees, with the x-axis vertical and the y-axis horizontal.

Stacked   Displays corresponding data-range values in stacked form on selecting **Yes**. This feature can be used with line, bar, XY and mixed charts.

100%   Displays the corresponding data-range values as percentages of their total values on selecting **Yes**. This feature can be used with line, bar, XY, stacked bar, and mixed charts.

2Y-Ranges   Allows the display of charts on two y-axes. Selecting **Graph**, lets you assign all data ranges to the second y-axis, while selecting data ranges A - F lets you assign individual data ranges to the second y-axis.

Y-Range	Allows the reassignment of data ranges to the first y-axis. Selecting **Graph**, lets you reassign all data ranges, while selecting data ranges A - F lets you reassign individual data ranges to the first y-axis.
Frame	Allows the addition or removal of a frame around part or all of a graph.
Drop-Shadow	Allows the addition or removal of a drop shadow to any graph except the HLCO type.
3D	Allows three-dimensional chart representation with all graphs except the HLCO type.
Table	Allows the display of a table of graph values below the graph when used with the line, bar, stacked bar, or mixed chart types.

Graphs can only be displayed at the same time as the worksheet if the Wysiwyg add-in is invoked, because graphs use the graphics mode of your computer while worksheets use the text mode, unless viewed through the Wysiwyg add-in. Nevertheless, irrespective of which mode of the program you are using, once the preliminary definition of data is made and selection of the type of graph you would like to see is made, viewing a graph is very easy. Furthermore, as graphs are dynamic, any changes made to the data are automatically reflected on the defined graphs.

Preparing for a Line Graph:
In order to illustrate some of the graphing capabilities of Lotus 1-2-3, we will now plot the income of the consulting company we discussed in the PROJECT3 file. However, before we can go on, you will need to activate the 'Window Perspective' SmartIcon (the 2nd of palette 5) in order to display the consolidation sheet A in full screen. Then you need to complete the entries for the last two quarters of trading of the Adept Consultants' example, if you haven't already done so, and link the quarterly totals to the consolidation sheet, which now should look as shown overleaf.

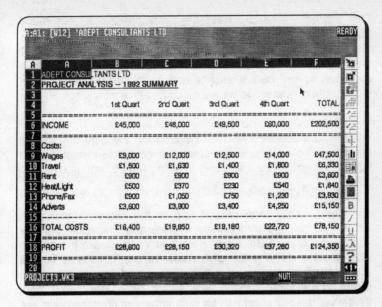

A	A	B	C	D	E	F
1	ADEPT CONSULTANTS LTD					
2	PROJECT ANALYSIS – 1992 SUMMARY					
3						
4		1st Quart	2nd Quart	3rd Quart	4th Quart	TOTAL
5						
6	INCOME	£45,000	£48,000	£49,500	£60,000	£202,500
7						
8	Costs:					
9	Wages	£9,000	£12,000	£12,500	£14,000	£47,500
10	Travel	£1,500	£1,630	£1,400	£1,800	£6,330
11	Rent	£900	£900	£900	£900	£3,600
12	Heat/Light	£500	£370	£230	£540	£1,640
13	Phone/Fax	£900	£1,050	£750	£1,230	£3,930
14	Adverts	£3,600	£3,900	£3,400	£4,250	£15,150
15						
16	TOTAL COSTS	£16,400	£19,850	£19,180	£22,720	£78,150
17						
18	PROFIT	£28,600	£28,150	£30,320	£37,280	£124,350
19						
20						

PROJECT3.WK3

Of course, if you don't feel like doing this right now, you can always create a new worksheet which includes the values of the consolidation sheet, as shown above. However, for those who would like to do things properly, we list below the data used in creating it. Save the result as PROJECT4.

	Jul	Aug	Sep	Oct	Nov	Dec
Income	17,000	16,000	16,500	18,000	20,000	22,000
Costs:						
Wages	4,000	4,000	4,500	4,000	4,500	5,500
Travel	450	400	550	550	600	650
Rent	300	300	300	300	300	300
Heat/Light	80	60	90	130	170	240
Phone/Fax	330	170	250	380	400	450
Adverts	1,200	1,000	1,200	1,350	1,400	1,500

First we need to define the type of graph to be displayed, followed by the range of the data we want to graph. Luckily, the range of data to be graphed is contiguous for each graph, otherwise we would have had to create an appropriate contiguous data range in another area of the worksheet. This could be done by either referencing the necessary sheet cells with a + sign, or by using the /**Range, Value** command, which copies a range and converts formulae to values.

The former method has the advantage of automatic recalculation should any changes be made to the original data. Cells containing formulae, cannot be copied using the /**Copy** only command since it would cause the relative cell addresses to adjust to the new locations and each formula would then recalculate a new value for each cell and give wrong results.

The /Graph Command:
We can now proceed with the definition of the type of graph to be drawn. To do this, make sure that the mode indicator is on READY, then ZOOM into sheet A, using Alt+**F6**, and use the

/Graph, Type, Line

command. Lotus then returns you to the 'Graph' menu from which you can specify the X data-range as A:B4..A:E4, and the A data-range as A:B6..A:E6. Selecting **View**, clears the screen and displays a line graph of 'Income' versus 'Quarters'. To see a bar chart of the same information, simply press <Esc> to return to the 'Graph' menu, and select **Type, Bar, View**. With Wysiwyg, the bar-chart can be superimposed on the worksheet, as shown below:

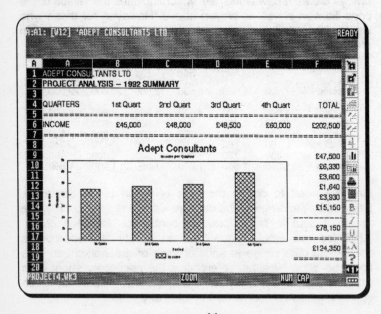

44

To achieve this, use the Wysiwyg

:Graph, Add, Current

command, specify A:A8..A:E10 as the range where you would like to see the graph, and press <Enter>. With the mouse, point to cell A:A8, click the left button, and while holding the button down, drag the mouse to highlight the required range, release the button and click once. The specified range on the worksheet clears and the current graph is drawn, as shown on the previous page.

You can change the type of graph by simply returning to the READY mode and selecting the /**Graph, Type** command and choosing a different type, say, Line. Try it, then change the first quarter income from £45,000 to £55,000 and watch how the change is reflected on the redrawn graph.

Naming Ranges and Graphs

It is often more convenient to 'name' a range of data and then use the name rather than the cell addresses in subsequent worksheet operations, including graphing. To illustrate this point, select the Wysiwyg

:Graph, Remove

command, point and click on the graph on the Wysiwyg screen and press <Enter> to remove it. Now return to the READY mode and type in cell A:A4 the label PERIOD, then use the

/Range, Name, Create

command, type PERIOD and specify range A:B4..E4 for this name.

Repeat the procedure to name INCOME as range A:B6..E6, then use the

/Graph, Reset, Ranges

command to clear remembered group ranges from the previous operations in graphing. Note that the named settings of the last created graph remain the current, and when you select new settings, the current ones are presented as default so that you can reuse as many of these as you like.

45

This reduces the time required to define new settings for a graph that happens to be rather similar to the one you have already defined. Next, select the /**Graph, Type, Line** command and type in for the X data-range the actual name PERIOD (don't select the label with the same name from the worksheet, as it will not work), and for the A data-range the name INCOME. Selecting the **View** command now displays the familiar line graph.

To name a graph, first specify a graph and view it, which makes it the 'current' graph, then use the

/**Graph, Name, Create**

command to give your current graph a name. If you have been following our suggested example so far, the current graph in memory is the Income line graph, so type the name INCOME_LINE. Other options available within the **Name** sub-menu allow you to **Use** (make a named graph current), **Delete** (a named graph), **Reset** (delete graphs, settings, or formats of named graphs in the current file), and **Table** (create a table of named graphs in the current file). Finally, use the /**Graph, Type** command, select the **Bar** option and then name it INCOME_BAR.

Saving Graphs:
Graphs and charts will only be saved under the particular spreadsheet in which they were created (so that they can be accessed at a later stage), if you name them and then, before quitting 1-2-3, you save the spreadsheet again under its given name. If you have already named the suggested graphs, save your spreadsheet under the filename PROJECT5. This will ensure that your named graphs are also saved with the spreadsheet. You can save as many separate graphs with the same spreadsheet filename as you like, provided you give each one a different name using the

/**Graph, Name, Create**

command. To select any graph and make it current, choose the **Name, Use** command (press the **F3** function key to see a list of saved chart names in tabular form, if you have defined lots of them), highlight the required one and press <Enter>.

The /**Graph, Save** command saves a current graph in a separate file on disc for use with other programs. Such saved graphs cannot be accessed by a worksheet, unless you load the Wysiwyg add-in, use the :**Graph, View** oommand and select the **Metafile** option.

Labels and Titles:
There are several options within the /**Graph, Options** sub-menu which allow you to add information to your graph, such as Legends, Titles, and Data-labels. The **Legend** option allows you to select up to six data-ranges for which you can specify the wording of a legend which then appears on the X-axis of your graph. In the case of our INCOME_LINE example, this would be 'Income'.

Having typed your preference for a legend, press <Esc> to return to the **Graph, Options** menu. Selecting the **Titles** option, invokes a sub-menu which allows you to add a 'First' and 'Second' title and annotate the X, Y1 and Y2 axes. Add the suggested titles so that what appears on your screen is as shown below:

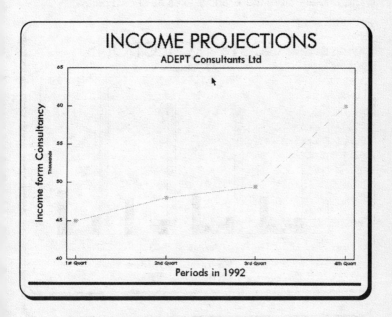

Selection of the /**Graph, Options, Advance** command, allows you to specify the colour or hatch pattern for each of the six data-ranges, and select text attributes for the titles and legends. Having made your selections, press <Esc> to return to the **Graph** menu, then select **View** to display the current graph with the latest changes. Finally, name the graph using the **Name, Create** command, then save your worksheet as PROJECT6.

Drawing a Multiple Bar Chart:
As an exercise, define graph settings for a new bar-type graph which deals with the quarterly 'Costs' of Adept Consultants. As there are six different contiguous sets of costs, shown against their cost description labels, you can select in succession data-ranges A - F, and define for each a different cost range.

In this way, 6 different bars (corresponding to the six different costs) can be plotted for each quarter, with appropriate legends so that the different cost categories can be distinguished clearly. Selecting legends for these costs can be done easily by selecting the **Range** option from the **Legend** sub-menu, and highlighting A:A9..A:A14. Then, give an appropriate title to your chart, and annotate the x- and y-axes as shown below:

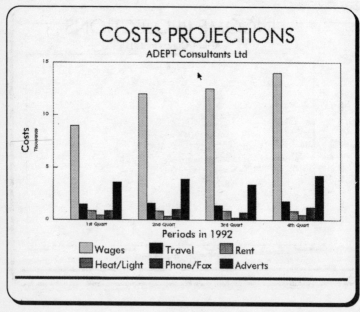

Finally, use the **Name, Create** command to give the graph the name COSTS_BAR, then save the graphs in the current worksheet by saving the spreadsheet, once again, under the filename PROJECT6.

Drawing a Pie Chart:

As a second example, use the 'Total' values of the costs from the spreadsheet of PROJECT6 to plot a pie chart. First, define the new graph type as 'Pie' and then specify the cell range A:A9..A:A14 as the X data-range and the cell range A:F9..A:F14 as the A data-range.

Since the bar chart representation of the various costs was the last defined series of ranges, the originally specified ranges for the X and A data-ranges are presented as the default values. These have to be cancelled by pressing <Esc> in order to be able to move the highlighted cell to the beginning of the new data ranges. Furthermore, specify cell range A:G9..A:G14 (which holds no values as yet) as the B data-range. On selecting the **View** option, the pie chart is drawn on screen with each cost slice appearing in a different colour. Selecting the **Options, B&W** command and viewing again the pie chart, it is now displayed as follows:

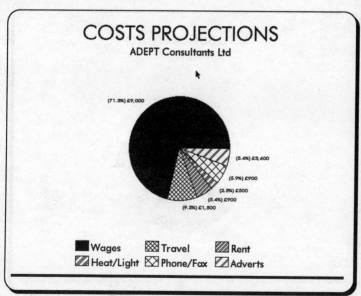

Lotus 1-2-3 uses the default colours or hatch patterns (if the **B&W** option has been invoked) to display the various pie slices, unless the B data-range is used to set these to different colours or hatch patterns. This can be done by entering a value from 1 to 14 on a cell range adjacent to the total costs range. A negative number hides the corresponding slice, while adding 100 to the chosen B value, explodes the corresponding slice. You can use the C data-range, to enter 0, in order to hide the percent labels displayed against each pie slice.

One way of creating automatically the required colour, or cross-hatching codes, is to exploit the **/Data, Fill** command. The command first asks for a range to be defined for data filling, which in your case should be A:G9..A:G14, and then asks for the Start, Step and Stop values of the data. Use 1, 1 and 6 for these and watch the specified range fill automatically with these numbers. Viewing the pie chart now in the **B&W** option, shows the cross-hatching of its different slices.

The pie chart shown below displays the available cross-hatching patterns against codes 1 to 14. The percent labels have been suppressed, and slice number 1 has been emphasized by detaching it from the rest of the pie chart by adding 100 to its code number.

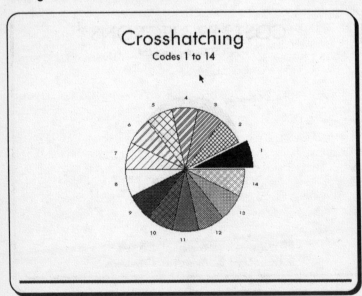

Crosshatching
Codes 1 to 14

Printing Data and Graphs

If you have changed your primary printer since first installing Lotus 1-2-3, select the

/Print, Printer, Options, Advanced, Device, Name

command which causes the program to list the available printers (specified during installation) against numbers (or numbers and letters, if you have installed more than nine printers) from which you can select the currently connected printer. If your printer is not listed, then quit 1-2-3 and invoke the Install program again.

Once the correct printer has been specified, you can send to it either a range of data from your worksheet or a graph, by selecting either the **/Print, Printer** command and choosing **Range** followed by the worksheet range, or the **Image** option and specifying the **Current** or a **Named-Graph.** Once the correct selection has been made, then choose the **Align, Go** command which sends output to your printer.

The **Align** command is needed so that 1-2-3 can correctly align headers and footers on paper. Without the **Align** command, you might get a misplaced page break in the middle of a printout. Both graphs and ranges can be printed in different orientation by selecting appropriate commands, as follows:

For a graph **/Print, Options, Advanced, Image, Rotate**

For a range **/Print, Options, Advanced, Layout, Orientation**

You can even change the size of graphs and the pitch of characters in a range, or even print both a range and a graph on the same piece of paper. The possibilities are endless.

If you would like to print information via a shared printer which is not connected to your computer, first print to a disc file, then use it later to transfer the information onto paper direct from the DOS prompt of the computer connected to the shared printer, as explained at the beginning of the previous chapter.

If you have the Wysiwyg add-in attached, you can use the **:Print, Range** command to specify a range, or ranges, of your worksheet which you would like to print. These can include embedded graphs. Having specified the range, you can first see on your screen what will be printed by selecting the **Preview** option, then send the output to the printer by selecting the **Go** command.

Printing with the Wysiwyg **:Print** command causes 1-2-3 to print from graphics mode which will then print any Wysiwyg formatting enhancements you have made to your work. Even with a 9 pin dot matrix printer you can get very impressive results. There is a penalty though, in that graphics mode printing can be much slower. If speed is more important than the quality of your output, we suggest you don't use Wysiwyg enhancements and print your spreadsheets through the **/Print** menu.

The Wysiwyg add-in includes a wealth of options which can be used to enhance the visual output of your work. These capabilities are so many, that they warrant separate discussion. This is done in the next chapter.

5. EXPLORING WYSIWYG

The Wysiwyg (what-you-see-is-what-you-get) add-in that comes with Lotus 1-2-3 (for other add-ins see Appendix D), allows you to enhance the appearance of your worksheet both on screen and on paper. Amongst other things, you can customise worksheet fonts, add text enhancements (such as italics, bold and underline), shade worksheet ranges, and change screen colours. The printed output that you can achieve with Wysiwyg is of very high quality, whether you print reports, documents or graphs. You can even name groups of formats used in a specific report as sheet styles, so that you can easily format ranges consistently with the same group of formats.

Loading Wysiwyg
Normally, the Wysiwyg module loads into memory automatically when you load 1-2-3; this is the default condition. However, if for some reason you have removed the module from memory, you will need to load it again so that you can benefit from what is presented here.

To load Wysiwyg into memory, first load 1-2-3, and when the program displays a blank worksheet and is in the READY mode, press ADDIN (Alt+**F10**) and select

    Load, WYSIWYG.PLC, **No-Key, Quit**

This way of loading Wysiwyg, as opposed to assigning it to one of the APP1 to APP3 (Alt+**F7** to Alt+**F9**) keys, allows you to use the colon (:) method for accessing the Wysiwyg menu. If you want Wysiwyg to load automatically whenever you load 1-2-3, then press ADDIN (Alt+**F10**) and select

    Settings, System, Set, WYSIWYG.PLC, **Yes, No-Key, Update**

Next time you load 1-2-3, Wysiwyg will be loaded automatically into memory, and invoked.

Selecting Wysiwyg Commands:
When Wysiwyg is active, the main Lotus 1-2-3 menu can be activated by pressing the slash (/) key. You can invoke the Wysiwyg menu, either by pressing the colon (:) key on the

keyboard (if you have loaded the program with the **No-Key** option), then selecting commands by typing their first letter, or by using the mouse, provided you have installed one first.

To invoke the main Lotus 1-2-3 menu with the mouse, simply move the mouse pointer into the control panel at the top of the screen. Pressing the right mouse button, toggles the menu between the main menu and the Wysiwyg menu. Selecting commands with the use of the mouse, from either menu, is a matter of pointing to a chosen command and pressing the left mouse button. Once a command has been chosen, pressing the right mouse button has the same effect as pressing <Esc> on the keyboard.

If you are a left-handed person and wish to switch the mouse buttons around so that the left button is used for the right (and vice versa), then use the Install program and select the Wysiwyg options. Other options can be used to generate fonts for printing and screen display, or add soft fonts from a disc to use with Wysiwyg.

To hide the displayed SmartIcon palette, either click the icon with the three small squares (under the palette number), or press Ctrl+**F9**. The screen dump below, shows the top-half of the screen when this is done.

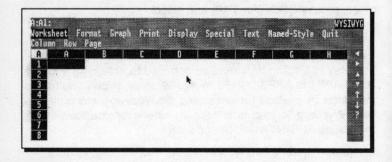

Mouse Shortcuts:
The seven icons on the right hand side of the above display can be used with the mouse to move the cell pointer left or right in the current worksheet (top two), move the cell pointer up or down in the current worksheet (next two), move the cell pointer forward or backward through worksheets (next two - long arrows), or invoke the help screen (last one).

Furthermore, you can use the mouse to create vertical or horizontal windows by pointing to the worksheet letter, pressing the left mouse button and dragging the mouse to the right or down, respectively, until the desired window size is reached, then release the mouse button. To clear such windows, move the mouse pointer to the worksheet letter of either window and drag the mouse right or down a small distance and back to the worksheet letter.

Finally, you can use the mouse to specify worksheet ranges when asked by the program, whether these are single-sheet or three-dimensional ranges. You can even specify a range before selecting a command which can prove useful when trying to apply a variety of formats to a range without having to specify the range for each command. These can be achieved as follows:

1. For a single-sheet range - move the mouse pointer to one corner of the range, click the left mouse button and drag the mouse to the opposite corner of the cell range, then release the mouse button. The range is highlighted and to specify it, click the left mouse button.

2. For a three-dimensional range - highlight the single-sheet range, following the steps in 1 above, then click the up arrow icon panel once (for each sheet you would like to include) to move forward to the next sheet (or the down arrow icon panel to move backwards to the previous sheet). The range is highlighted and to specify it, click the left mouse button.

3. For highlighting a range prior to selecting a command - move the cell pointer to one corner of the required range and press **F4** (or Ctrl and click the left mouse button), highlight the range, following the steps in 1 and/or 2 above, then select the command you want to use which causes 1-2-3 to carry out the command without asking for the range. The specified range remains highlighted (unless you move the cell pointer, press <Esc>, or click the left mouse button) ready for selecting the next command. When you have finished with all the commands, click the left mouse button.

The Wysiwyg Commands

There are eight commands in the main Wysiwyg menu which can be used to enhance what Lotus 1-2-3 displays, or prints. What these commands can achieve, are listed below in the order they appear on the main Wysiwyg menu.

:Worksheet is used to control the width of a column or a range of columns, the height of a row or a range of rows, and to insert or remove a page break.

:Format is used to format worksheet data in any of eight fonts, add text enhancements such as bold, italics, or underline, select a different colour for a range, add a variety of horizontal and vertical lines to a range, including drop shadows, and shade a range.

:Graph is used to place 1-2-3 graphs anywhere in a worksheet, and then enhance them with colours, text, arrows, and geometric shapes. You can even view and add external graph files saved under the .PIC and .CGM formats, or create free-hand drawings and annotations.

:Print is used to specify the printer, interface and font cartridges, orientation and resolution of the output, paper type and size, margins, titles, headers, footers and preview a printed range on screen.

:Display is used to customise the screen display by selecting between graphics and text mode, B&W and colour, selecting between six different sizes of zoom, choosing the colours for the worksheet background and data, specifying the cell pointer style between solid or outline, and adding grid lines to the worksheet.

:Special is used to copy or move the format of a range to another range, import the format and/or settings of another worksheet to the current file, and export formatting information to disc in a .FM3, .FMT, or .ALL format.

:Text is used to enter information in a worksheet as if you were using a word processor. Data can be entered directly in a range (instead of in the control panel) with word wrap, font and formatting control. Text alignment is within the specified range (instead of within cells).

:Named-Style is used to assign names to groups of formats by defining up to eight such groups, so that you can later format easily and consistently other worksheet ranges with the same group of formats.

To illustrate some of the capabilities of Wysiwyg, we will use the PROJECT6 file (see end of previous chapter) to first import the COSTS_PIE chart into a range of the worksheet, then we will format and enhance the actual worksheet data layout, before we print both, on the same page, in report form. This will be carried out step by step, each time printing a more enhanced report, in order to cover as many Wysiwyg enhancing commands as possible.

Start by retrieving the worksheet PROJECT6 and then use the

:Graph, Add, Named

command to select COSTS_PIE and specify the range A:B21..A:E45 by highlighting it. It is important that you choose a squarish area into which to import your graph, otherwise the pie chart instead of printing as a circle will print as an ellipse. Next, use the

:Print, Range, Set

command and specify cell range A:A1..A:F46, followed by the

Layout, Page-Size

command and choose option **2:A4** for the paper size, followed by the

Titles, Header

option, and typing the words 'Income & Expenditure Report', followed by the **Footer** option, and typing the text 'January 1993||Page#'. The Print definition page should now look as follows:

```
Print range(s).... A:A1..A:F46          Margins (in inches)

Layout:                                           Top 0.5
   Paper type... A4
   Page size.... 8.268 by 11.693 inches
   Titles:                               Left               Right
      Header..... Income & Expenditure Repo... 0.5          0.5
      Footer..... January 1993||Page#
   Top border...
   Left border..                                 Bottom 0.55
   Compression.. None
                                         Settings:
Configuration:                              Begin......... 1
   Printer...... Apple LaserWriter Plus Ti...    End........... 9999
   Interface.... Parallel 1                      Start-Number.. 1
   Cartridges...                                 Copies........ 1
   Orientation.. Portrait                        Wait.......... No
   Resolution... Final                           Grid.......... No
   Bin..........                                 Frame......... No

REPORT1.WK3                    ZOOM                      NUM
```

There are four special characters that can be used to format
printed information. The vertical bar (|) is used to separate
left-aligned, centred, and right-aligned portions of a header or
footer, the hash sign (#) indicates a page number, the at sign
(@) indicates the current date, and the backslash (\) followed
by a cell address can be used to copy cell contents to the
header or footer.

   You can preview the layout of your work so far, on a full page
display, by selecting the **Preview** option, and/or you can print it
on paper by selecting the **Go** command. If you issue the **Go**
command while your printer is disconnected, then you must use
the

   /Print, Resume

or the

   /Print, Cancel

command to clear the printer queue. The printout should look
as follows:

58

ADEPT CONSULTANTS LTD
PROJECT ANALYSIS - 1992 SUMMARY

PERIOD	1st Quart	2nd Quart	3rd Quart	4th Quart	TOTAL
INCOME	£45,000	£48,000	£49,500	£60,000	£202,500
Costs:					
Wages	£9,000	£12,000	£12,500	£14,000	£47,500
Travel	£1,500	£1,630	£1,400	£1,800	£6,330
Rent	£900	£900	£900	£900	£3,600
Heat/Light	£500	£370	£230	£540	£1,640
Phone/Fax	£900	£1,050	£750	£1,230	£3,930
Adverts	£3,600	£3,900	£3,400	£4,250	£3,600
TOTAL COSTS	£16,400	£19,850	£19,180	£22,720	£66,600
PROFIT	£28,600	£28,150	£30,320	£37,280	£135,900

COSTS PROJECTIONS
ADEPT Consultants Ltd

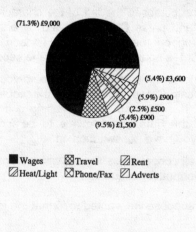

(71.3%) £9,000
(5.4%) £3,600
(5.9%) £900
(2.5%) £500
(5.4%) £900
(9.5%) £1,500

■ Wages ⊠ Travel ⧅ Rent
⧄ Heat/Light ⊠ Phone/Fax ⧄ Adverts

Obviously, before this report becomes acceptable we need to use quite a bit of cosmetic surgery, particularly on the layout of the worksheet data. You might also need to look at the default type styles available with Wysiwyg which might not be available to your printer. However, before we start doing so, save the current worksheet under the filename REPORT1.

Formatting Sequences

When you need to format specific characters you have inserted in a cell, or text you have typed in headers and footers, or format text you have added to a graphic using the Wysiwyg **:Graph, Edit, Add** command, then you must use the special formatting sequence codes, listed in the table below, because these enhancements cannot be done through the menu system.

To enhance such characters or text, as mentioned above, carry out the procedure outlined below, but do remember that formatting codes are case sensitive, therefore you must make sure you use the appropriate case letter exactly as it appears in the table. Further, as more than one code can be applied to a set of characters at a time, there is a facility to switch off one code or more codes and carry on formatting with the rest, or end all formatting codes at once. Thus, to start a formatting sequence

- place the cursor to the left of the character you want to format and press Ctrl+**a**, followed by one of the codes appearing on the table below. To add another code, press Ctrl+**a** again and follow it by the second code.

- move the cursor to the end of the data you are formatting and press Ctrl+**e** followed by the code you want to cancel. If more than one formatting code is active, the rest of the data can continue to be formatted by the codes you have not switched off.

- to end all codes, press Ctrl+**n**, which also marks the end of the formatting sequence.

For example, suppose we wanted to format the following text as shown:

Formatting when you can't use a menu

with the whole text in bold, italic, but the first word underlined as well, then move the cursor to the left of the first character (F in this case), and press Ctrl+**a** then type b; then press Ctrl+**a** then type i; then press Ctrl+**a** and type 1_. Next, move the cursor to the right of _g_ and press Ctrl+**e** then type 1_ to end underlining. Finally, move the cursor to the end of the text and press Ctrl+**n**.

60

Note: Do not use cells containing formatted labels to create range names, as unexpected results may occur.

Code	Format
b	Bold
d	Subscript
i	Italics
u	Superscript
x	Data flipped on its x-axis (backwards)
y	Data flipped on its y-axis (upside down)
1_	Single underlining
2_	Double underlining
3_	Wide underlining
5_	Outline around characters
1c	Default colour set with **:Display, Colors, Text**
2c	Red
3c	Green
4c	Dark blue
5c	Cyan
6c	Yellow
7c	Magenta
8c	Reversed colours for data and background
1F and A	Font 1 from the current font set
2F and B	Font 2 from the current font set
3F and C	Font 3 from the current font set
4F and D	Font 4 from the current font set
5F and E	Font 5 from the current font set
6F and F	Font 6 from the current font set
7F and G	Font 7 from the current font set
8F and H	Font 8 from the current font set
1g to 6g	Shades of grey
1k to 127k	Spacing between characters
1o to 255o	Outline of characters
1r to 3r	Rotated text.

To remove formatting sequences, move the cell pointer to the cell that contains the formatting sequence and press **F2** (EDIT) to display the formatting sequence in the control panel, and use the <Del> or <BkSp> key to remove the formatting sequence characters.

Wysiwyg Type Styles

When you use Wysiwyg for the first time, the eight fonts that you can use with a worksheet, called the font set, and accessed with the

:Format, Font

command, includes Swiss typeface in 12, 14, and 24 point size (selected with font options 1 to 3), Dutch typeface in 6, 8, 10, and 12 point size (selected with font options 4 to 7), and Xsymbol typeface in 12 point size (selected with font option 8). These fonts can be replaced by using the

:Format, Font, Replace

command, which allows you to replace any of the default fonts (1-8) with a typeface of your choice from **Swiss, Dutch, Courier, Xsymbol,** and **Other** (with the latter including a list of 18, mainly fonts used with a PostScript printer), with point sizes ranging from 3 to 72.

A 'point' is a unit of measurement, approximately 1/72 of an inch, that determines the height of a character. The spacing of a font is either 'fixed' (monospaced) or 'proportional'. With fixed spacing, each character takes up exactly the same space, while proportionally spaced characters take up different spacing (an i or a t take up less space than a u or a w). Thus the length of proportionally spaced text can vary depending on which letters it contains. However, numerals take up the same amount of space whether they have been specified as fixed or proportional.

Which fonts you choose is largely dependent on your printer. Here you can experiment to your heart's delight, but it will take time. One thing you must bear in mind is that 1-2-3 uses screen fonts to display characters on screen and printer fonts to print characters with a printer. If you choose printer fonts for which there are no screen fonts, 1-2-3 will use the nearest screen font to display your work on screen, which might not be exactly what you will see when you print your work. Furthermore, even if you choose the correct character fonts for your printer, 1-2-3 will use your printer's graphics capability to print your work when you select the

:Print, Go

commaiid producing an inferior output. If, on the other hand you select the

/Print, Printer, Go

command (you will have to specify the **Range** again), the output will be at its best for your particular printer, but since it was printed in text form, the graph in the included range will not be printed.

Best output results can only be obtained when using a laser printer with PostScript capability. So, if you want to produce high-quality reports, and you have access to a PostScript printer, then use the Install program to install it as a second printer, then select the

:Print, Configuration, Printer

command to make it the current printer. From then on, use the **:Print, File** command which sends print output to an encoded file on disc. Such a file can be printed on your laser printer by using the DOS command

COPY *Filename.Ext* LPT1

on the computer connected to it, without needing the 1-2-3 program, as discussed at the beginning of Chapter 3.

Wysiwyg Formatting

We shall now use various Wysiwyg formatting commands to improve the looks of the 1992 report on Adept Consultants Ltd. We carry out the following improvements:

1. Delete row 1 of the worksheet by using the **/Worksheet, Delete** command.

2. Add the text '||ADEPT Consultants Ltd' to the report header, using the **:Print, Layout, Titles, Header** command so that the additions appear on the extreme right-hand side of the printed page.

3. Replace the equals and minus signs now appearing in rows 4, 6, 14, 16, and 18, by first erasing the contents of each of the specified rows using the **/Range, Erase** command, then use the **:Worksheet, Row, Set-Height** command to set the height of each of the specified rows to 5 points. Next, use the **:Format, Lines, Double, Top** command to draw double horizontal lines at the top edge of each cell in the range for all the specified rows, except row 14. For row 14 use a single horizontal line at the top edge of each cell in the required range.

4. Centre the report title (in A:A1) by using the **:Text, Align, Center** command and specifying A:A1..A:F1 as the range within which it is to be aligned. Next, use the **:Text, Set** command to set the range to be used with the **Edit** option, press <Enter> to accept the displayed edit range. Now select **:Text, Edit,** <Enter>, and press NAME (**F3**) to reveal a sub-menu from which choose **Italics,** followed by NAME (**F3**) to reveal the sub-menu again, and choose **Outline.** Finally, press <Esc> to return to the READY mode.

Save the result as REPORT2. The top-half of your worksheet should now look as follows:

5. Remove the graph from the display by using the **:Graph, Remove** command, then remove the second line of the graph title by using the **/Graph, Options, Titles, Second** command, backspacing to delete the displayed text and pressing <Enter>, then selecting the **/Graph, Options, Advanced, Text, First, Size** command and specifying text size **5**. Next, use the **:Graph, Add** command to reinsert the edited pie chart in range A:B20..A:F49 (note the increased range).

    Note that 1-2-3 displays graph text in three sizes, therefore select settings 1-3 for small-size text, 4-6 for medium-size text, and 7-9 for large-size text. The **Default** settings are 8, 4, and 2 for the first, second, and third graph-text groups, respectively.

6. Add text to the graph portion of the display by first using the **:Graph, Goto** command to move to the beginning of the graph area (in this case A:B20), then selecting the **:Graph, Edit** command, specifying the graphic to edit as A:B20 by pressing <Enter>, choosing the **Add, Text** option and typing the text 'For Year 1992'. Place the text in the graph, centrally positioned, under its main caption, then use the options **Add, Line** and **Add, Arrow** to add a horizontal line and an inclined arrow, as shown below. Save the result as REPORT3.

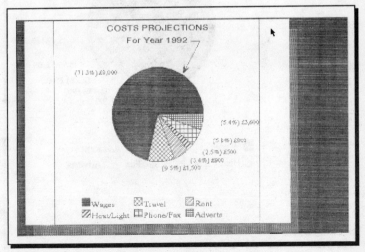

7. Finally, use the **:Format, Shade, Light** command and specify the range to be shaded lightly as A:F3..A:F17, and save the result as REPORT4. The printout (range A:A1..A:F50), using a PostScript printer, is shown below.

Income & Expenditure Report   ADEPT Consultants Ltd

PROJECT ANALYSIS - 1992 SUMMARY

PERIOD	1st Quart	2nd Quart	3rd Quart	4th Quart	TOTAL
INCOME	£45,000	£48,000	£49,500	£60,000	£202,500
Costs:					
Wages	£9,000	£12,000	£12,500	£14,000	£47,500
Travel	£1,500	£1,630	£1,400	£1,800	£6,330
Rent	£900	£900	£900	£900	£3,600
Heat/Light	£500	£370	£230	£540	£1,640
Phone/Fax	£900	£1,050	£750	£1,230	£3,930
Adverts	£3,600	£3,900	£3,400	£4,250	£3,600
TOTAL COSTS	£16,400	£19,850	£19,180	£22,720	£66,600
PROFIT	£28,600	£28,150	£30,320	£37,280	£135,900

COSTS PROJECTIONS
For Year 1992

(71.3%) £9,000

(5.4%) £3,600

(5.9%) £900

(2.5%) £500

(5.4%) £900

(9.5%) £1,500

■ Wages   ⊠ Travel   ▨ Rent
▨ Heat/Light   ⊠ Phone/Fax   ▨ Adverts

Note: Objects within a graphic window (which can be a line of text, a geometric shape, or a free-hand drawing) that you have added with the **:Graph, Edit** commands, can be edited, moved or removed. However, before you can carry out any of these commands, you must 'select', or identify such objects using the **:Graph, Edit, Select** command (or when using the mouse, by pointing to the required object and double clicking the left mouse button). When an object has been selected, small filled squares appear on its outer edges. You can move such objects by pointing to one of the small filled squares and dragging them to a new position.

1-2-3 Commands Affecting Wysiwyg:

There are several 1-2-3 commands that affect Wysiwyg formatting. These are listed below in alphabetical order.

/Copy

When you use this command to copy a range of data, 1-2-3 copies all Wysiwyg formatting except lines and drop shadows added with the **:Format, Lines** command, or named style definitions. To copy updated or redefined named styles, use the **:Special, Copy** command.

/Data, Parse

Selecting this command, when Wysiwyg is in graphics display mode, puts Wysiwyg in text mode. Selecting **Quit**, from this command's sub-menu, returns Wysiwyg to graphics mode.

/Data, Sort

When this command is executed, all Wysiwyg formatting moves with the data except lines and drop shadows added with the **:Format, Lines** command.

/File, Combine

Combining a file from disc into the current file, does not bring formatting information into memory from a corresponding format file.

/File, Erase, Worksheet

Using this command erases a file from disc, together with its corresponding Wysiwyg (.FM3), Impress (.FMT), or (.ALL) format file, if they exist.

/File, New

When you use this command to create a new file in memory, the new file is created with the default font set, named styles, layout settings, and print configuration settings, except for Printer and Interface.

/File, Open and /File, Retrieve

Using these commands to read a .WK3 file, causes 1-2-3 to read the formatting information into memory from the Wysiwyg format file (.FM3) of the same name, if one exists. When the commands are used to read a .WK1 file, 1-2-3 reads formatting information from either a (.FMT) or a (.ALL) format file, if one exists; priority is given to the .FMT format file, if both a .FMT and a .ALL format files exist with the same name.

Files are read with the default print configuration settings except Printer and Interface, and print settings except Frame and Grid. The display settings remain unchanged except for negative-value colours, lines, and drop shadows.

/File, Save

Saving a .WK3 file, causes 1-2-3 to save formatting information in a Wysiwyg format file of the same name, but with an .FM3 extension. Saving a worksheet as a .WK1 file, saves formatting information in a .FMT file. To save formatting information in an Allways format file (.ALL), use the :Special, Export command.

/File, Xtract

When you use this command to extract data from an active file and save the extracted information on disc, 1-2-3 does not create a corresponding format file.

/Move

Using this command to move a range of data also moves all formats associated with the specified range.

/Worksheet, Erase

When you use this command to remove all active files from memory, 1-2-3 reverts to the default font set, named styles, layout settings, and print settings.

/Worksheet, Global, Group, Enable

Using this command to turn GROUP mode on, causes 1-2-3 to apply all formats set in the current worksheet with the **Format, Named-Style**, and **Text** commands, page breaks set with the **:Worksheet, Page** command, and all column and row widths set by the **:Worksheet, Column** and **:Worksheet, Row** commands, to all worksheets in the current file.

/Worksheet, Insert

Inserting columns or rows in a worksheet, causes 1-2-3 to format the new columns or rows with the Wysiwyg formats common to the columns or rows directly on either side of them.

/Worksheet, Window, Map, Enable

Selecting this command when Wysiwyg is in graphics display mode, puts Wysiwyg into text mode. Pressing <Esc> or <Enter> from map view, returns Wysiwyg to graphics display mode.

Removing Wysiwyg from Memory:

Wysiwyg can be removed from memory by pressing ADDIN (Alt+**F10**) and selecting **Remove.** However, before removing Wysiwyg from memory make sure you save your work with the **/File, Save** command, otherwise all formatting information will be lost.

* * *

Wysiwyg has many more commands that you can use to produce more professional-looking reports. In fact, one could devote a whole book to Wysiwyg. Nevertheless, we feel that what little has been discussed here, will form a good foundation from which to explore the package and add to your knowledge.

* * *

6. THE LOTUS 1-2-3 DATABASE

A 1-2-3 database table is a worksheet range which contains related information, such as 'Customer's Names', 'Consultancy Details', 'Invoice No.', etc. A phone book is a simple database table, stored on paper. In Lotus 1-2-3 each record is entered as a worksheet row, with the fields of each record occupying corresponding columns.

A database table is a collection of data that exists, and is organised around a specific theme or requirement. It is used for storing information so that it is quickly accessible. To make accessing the data easier, each row, or **record,** of data within a database table is structured in the same fashion, i.e. each record will have the same number of columns or **fields**.

We define a database and its various elements as follows:

Database table   A collection of related data organised in rows and columns in a worksheet file. A worksheet file can contain many different database tables

Record   A row of information relating to a single entry and comprising one or more fields

Field   A single column of information of the same type, such as people's names

Creating a Database

In order to investigate the various database functions, such as sorting, searching, etc., we first need to set-up a database table in the form shown overleaf.

Note that in creating a database table, the following rules must be observed:

1. The top row of the database table must contain the field labels, one per column, which identify the fields in the database table. The second and subsequent rows of such a database table must contain records; no blank rows should be inserted between the field labels and the records.

2. Field labels must be unique within a given database table.

3. Entries under each field must be of the same type.

4. A database table can contain a maximum of 256 fields and 8,191 records.

We assume that the 'Invoice Analysis' of Adept Consultants is designed and set out as shown below with the listed field titles and field widths. Formatting information is given below.

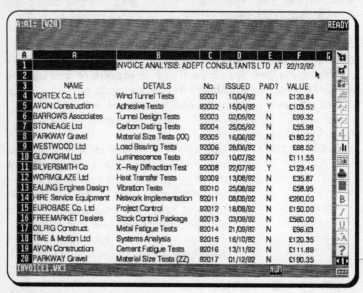

Use the /**Worksheet, Column, Set-Width** command to change the width of the various columns to those given below, and then enter the abbreviated titles, centrally positioned, in row 3, as shown in the worksheet above. These widths were chosen so that the whole worksheet could be seen on the screen at once.

Column	Title	Width	Type
A	NAME	20	Default
B	DETAILS	20	Default
C	No.	5	Fixed, 0 decimal
D	ISSUED	9	Date, type 4
E	PAID?	6	Default
F	VALUE	8	Currency, 2 decimal

Use the /**Range, Format, Fixed** command to format column C, and the /**Range, Format, Currency** command to format column F, before entering the numeric information. Finally, save the resultant worksheet under the filename INVOICE1.

Sorting a Database Table:

The records within the above database table are in the order in which they were entered, with the 'Invoice No' shown in ascending order. However, we might find it easier to browse through the information if it was sorted in alphabetical order of 'Customer's Name'. Lotus 1-2-3 has an easy way to do this.

To use it, place the highlighted bar at the beginning of the sort range (in this case A:A4 - don't include the title line in the range to be sorted), then select the

/Data, Sort, Data-Range

command, highlight the sort range (A:A4..A:F20) and press <Enter> to confirm range selection. Next, use **Primary-Key**, press <Enter> to confirm range selection and choose **A** for ascending sort order, followed by <Enter>. Finally, select **Secondary-Key**, highlight cell A:C4, press <Enter> to confirm sort order and choose **A** for ascending order, followed by <Enter> and **Go**. This produces the following display:

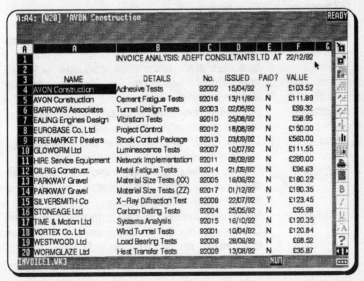

73

If you now decide to have an **Extra-Key** sort field, you don't even have to confirm the sort block range or the primary and secondary sort fields, as 1-2-3 remembers these. If you want to reset any of these 'remembered' ranges, then choose the appropriate sort function and press <Esc> to allow redefinition of the specific choice.

Now resort the database table in ascending order of 'Invoice No.' so that you obtain a display corresponding to the original data entry screen.

The /Data Query Command

The 9 commands under the /**Data, Query** command, are used to find specific records in a database table. However, before you can use any of these commands you must create at least two data query ranges; the input range and the criteria range. The input range defines your database table, while the criteria range is where you define the criteria under which the database table is to be searched. If you use any commands which copy selected records from the database table to another worksheet range, then you must also define an output range.

The various query commands and their description are listed below in order of appearance.

Command	Description
Input	Specifies the range, ranges, or external tables that contain the records you want to manipulate
Criteria	Specifies the range that contains selected criteria for searching or manipulating a database table
Output	Specifies the range where you want the results of a query to be placed
Find	Locates the records in the input range that match the criteria in the criteria range
Extract	Copies to the output range those records from the input range that match the criteria specified in the criteria range
Unique	Sorts and copies to the output range those unique records (omits duplicate records) from the input range that match the criteria specified in the criteria range

Del	Deletes the records in the input range that match the criteria in the criteria range
Modify	Inserts new records, or replaces modified records in the input range
Reset	Clears the settings for the input, criteria, and output ranges.

To illustrate how some of the above commands work, we assume that the database table of worksheet INVOICE1 is on your screen. If not, retrieve it from disc, then use the

/Worksheet, Global, Group, Enable

command, so that any formatting changes made to the current worksheet (the database table) will be reflected in corresponding areas of every worksheet in the current file. This causes the GROUP status indicator to be displayed at the bottom of the sheet, and allows us to insert one sheet after the current sheet, using the

/Worksheet, Insert, Sheet, After, 1

command, which will have the same column widths as the database table.

We shall then use part of the newly inserted sheet as our criteria range, but first we need to copy the field names of the database table, to be found in cell range A:A3..A:F3, into range B:A3..B:F3 of sheet B. This will form the first line of the criteria range. Next, type in cell A:A2 the label INPUT RANGE and in B:B2 the label CRITERIA RANGE, then use the

/Range, Name, Create

command to create the range name INPUT_R by highlighting cells A:A3..A:F20 and the range name CRITERIA_R by highlighting cells B:A3..B:F8, respectively.

Finally, we need to let 1-2-3 know the input and criteria ranges to be used when querying the database table, by selecting the

/Data, Query, Input

and

/Data, Query, Criteria

commands and specifying the names INPUT_R and
CRITERIA_R, respectively. Note that we have chosen the
method of giving range names to appropriate cells, so that
reference to such cells in, say, the 'input' and 'criteria'
declarations, is made by name rather than discrete cell
addressing.

The /Data Query Find Command:
The criteria must be entered in the second and subsequent
rows of the criteria range, with each criterion entered below the
copy of the appropriate field name. A label or a value may be
entered exactly as it appears in the database, or the two special
characters ? and * can be used to match any single character of
a label or all characters to the end of the label. Preceding a
label with a tilde (~), causes the search of all labels except for
that one. Thus, ~Y* searches the database for all records with
an entry in that field which does not begin with Y.

Thus, to search the database table for all the details of our
customers whose invoices have not been paid, type in cell B:E4
the criterion ~Y, then use the

/Data, Query, Find

command which will highlight the first record in the database
table that satisfies the typed criterion. Pressing the down-arrow
key highlights the next record that matches the chosen criteria.
If there are no more records, 1-2-3 bleeps. You can peruse
through the chosen records backwards by pressing the up
arrow key. Again, if there are no more records that match the
chosen criteria, 1-2-3 bleeps when the up arrow key is pressed.

To search a database for values, either enter the value as the
exact criterion or use a formula, such as

+A:F4>=100

in which the logical operators (<, <=, >, >=, <>) can be used.
The logical formula generates a value of 1 if the condition is
TRUE or a value of 0 if the condition is FALSE. This value
appears in the criterion range, unless the specific cell
containing the formula is formatted as 'text', by first using the

/Worksheet, Global, Group, Disable

command, to switch group formatting off, and then using the

/Range, Format, Text

command, in which case the actual formula (or part of it - depending on the width of the cell) will appear in the corresponding criterion cell. Note that a formula must specify the row of the first record in the database table, and not the row that contains field names.

Several criteria can be entered, either in the same row, if you want 1-2-3 to search for records that match every criterion (i.e. criteria entered are linked with the logical AND), or one per row, if you want 1-2-3 to search records that satisfy any of the criteria (i.e. criteria entered are linked with the logical OR). Compounded logical formulae can be used to create compound criteria that match more than one condition in the same field by using #AND#, #OR# or #NOT# in the formula. For example, had we typed the criterion in B:F4 as

    +A:F4>=100#AND#+A:F4<120

we would retrieve records whose values lie between £100 and £119.99. In our database table there are only two such records, one with invoice number 92007 and the other with invoice number 92016.

Note: Unwanted criteria must be removed from the criteria range by erasing them, using the **/Range, Erase** command, rather than over-typing them with spaces. A space has a value equal to zero and searching records with such a criterion will inevitably lead to errors.

The /Data Query Extract Command:
The **/Data, Query, Extract** command copies records that match the chosen criteria from the database table to the specified output range of the worksheet. First, copy the label and field names in cell range B:A2..B:F4 into B:A9..B:F10 and edit the contents of cell B:A9 to OUTPUT RANGE. Then use the

/Range, Name, Create

command to specify range B:A10..B:F10 as OUTPUT_R, followed by the

/Data, Query, Output

command to specify the output range into which data is to be copied as OUTPUT_R.

It is imperative that the area below the output range is sufficiently long to accommodate all the extracted records. In our example, this condition is met as we have chosen the output area to be below the criteria range in the B sheet. Specifying the output range by only the row of field names, causes the entire area under these field names to be cleared before the extracted records are copied into the output range. So, beware! If an output range of more than one row is specified, 1-2-3 does not erase the contents of the worksheet below the output range, but if such a multiple-row output range is not large enough to contain all the records that meet the criteria, an error message will be displayed.

The criteria we used previously with the /**Data, Query, Find** command were such that 2 records were found, therefore, using the

/Data, Query, Extract

command should extract the same two records, shown below.

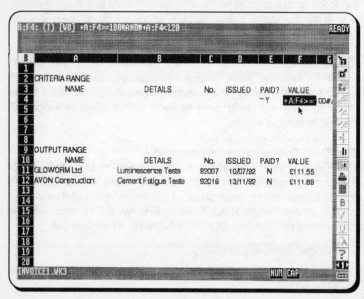

When the /**Data, Query, Extract** command is being executed, the CALC indicator appears in the lower right corner of the screen. After the selected records have been copied into the output range, the CALC indicator disappears. Pressing <Esc> three times, returns you to the READY mode at which point save the worksheet under the filename INVOICE2.

The /Data Query Modify Command:
This command lets you extract records from a database table by using the

/**Data, Query, Modify, Extract**

command, modify these records, and return them to the input range by using the

/**Data, Query, Modify, Replace**

command. You can also use the

/**Data, Query, Modify, Insert**

command to insert records you created in the output range into the input range.

To illustrate these commands, we will use the example in worksheet INVOICE2 to extract to the output range records by their invoice number, modify these records and return them to the input range. To begin with, erase the criterion under the VALUE field in cell B:F4, by using the /**Range, Erase** command, then insert the criterion ~Y in B:E5 and the two invoice numbers, say, 92005 and 92017, whose corresponding records we wish to modify, in cells B:C4 and B:C5, respectively. Now use the

/**Data, Query, Modify, Extract**

command and change cells B:E11 and B:E12 of the extracted records in the output range from N to Y, as shown on the next page.

Next, save your worksheet under the filename INVOICE3 and then, use the

/**Data, Query, Modify, Replace**

command to have the modified extracted records replace those in the input range.

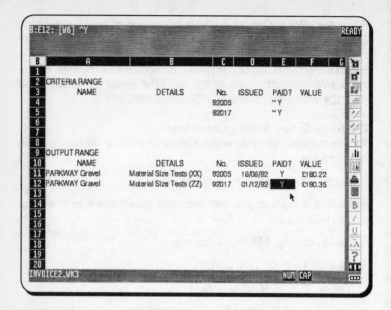

You can verify that this has been done by attempting to extract the same two records from the input range; no records will be extracted.

Date Arithmetic

There are several date functions which can be used in 1-2-3 to carry out date calculations. For example, typing the function @DATE(92,12,22) - 22/12/92 backwards - works out the number of days since 31 December 1899, while typing @NOW (as in cell A:G1 of the INVOICE2 worksheet), returns values which are dependent on the cell format. For example, if the cell is formatted as General, the function returns the number of days (in decimal) since the beginning of the century, but using the internal clock; the decimal part has to do with time. If, on the other hand, the cell is formatted as D4, the function returns the date in familiar form.

Another function, the @DATEVALUE, allows a date entered in the declared format of the spreadsheet (such as 10/4/90) to be used for calculations. Thus, typing

@NOW-@DATEVALUE("10/4/92") or
@NOW-@DATEVALUE(D4)

80

gives the difference in days (if the worksheet cell is formatted for integer numbers) between now and the mentioned date.

We can use these two functions to work out the number of overdue days of unpaid invoices in the database table of our example, but before doing so, we must change the layout of sheet B. First, retrieve INVOICE3 and make sure the GROUP mode is disabled, then delete column B, which deals with the invoicing details in the criteria and output ranges of sheet B, then type in cell B:F10 the formula

@DATEVALUE(A:$F$1)-@DATEVALUE(A:D4)

and format this cell as 'text' so that the actual formula can be seen. Next, use the /**Range, Name, Create** command to redefine the OUTPUT_R range to include cell B:F10. Finally, erase the contents of cells below row 10, and format range B:F11..F20 as **Fixed** with **0** decimal places.

Note: When creating a computed column in the output range, the actual formula must be typed in the row where field names would normally be typed. Furthermore, the computed column formula can include any function except @AVG, @COUNT, @MIN, @MAX, @SUM, or any of the database @functions. These functions can be used, however, to create an 'aggregate' column in the output range. An aggregate column is a column in which 1-2-3 calculates a total for a group of related values.

If you now change the criterion in cell B:E4 to

+A:F4>=100

and select the

/**Data, Query, Extract**

command, the actual number of overdue days are calculated and displayed on screen automatically, as shown on the next page.

After making the above suggested changes to your worksheet, save the result under the filename INVOICE4.

We could have used the formula

@NOW-@DATEVALUE(A:D4)

in cell B:F10 instead of the one above, which makes reference to cell A:$F$1.

81

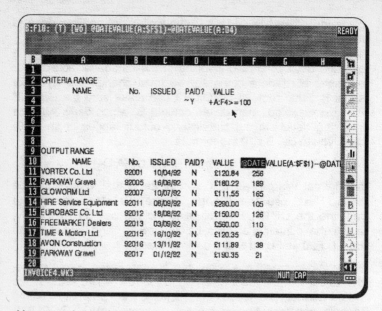

```
B:F10: (1) [W6] @DATEVALUE(A:$F$1)-@DATEVALUE(A:D4)          READY

 B        A          B      C       D      E       F        G        H
 1
 2  CRITERIA RANGE
 3         NAME          No.   ISSUED   PAID?   VALUE
 4                                       ~Y      +A:F4>=100
 5
 6
 7
 8
 9  OUTPUT RANGE
10         NAME          No.   ISSUED   PAID?   VALUE  @DATEVALUE(A:$F$1)-@DATE
11  VORTEX Co. Ltd      92001  10/04/92   N    £120.84   256
12  PARKWAY Gravel      92005  16/06/92   N    £180.22   189
13  GLOWORM Ltd         92007  10/07/92   N    £111.55   165
14  HIRE Service Equipment 92011 08/09/92 N    £290.00   105
15  EUROBASE Co. Ltd    92012  18/08/92   N    £150.00   126
16  FREEMARKET Dealers  92013  03/09/92   N    £560.00   110
17  TIME & Motion Ltd   92015  16/10/92   N    £120.35   67
18  AVON Construction   92016  13/11/92   N    £111.89   39
19  PARKWAY Gravel      92017  01/12/92   N    £190.35   21
20
INVOICE4.WK3                                          NUM CAP
```

However, be aware that using the @NOW function will give you results which will differ substantially from the ones shown above. The reason for this is that the @NOW function returns different numerical values when used at different dates. To get the same results as those shown above, replace the @NOW function in cell A:F1 with "22/12/92" and use the @DATEVALUE($F$1) version of the formula in cell B:F10.

WARNING: It is important that you enter the date, in cells which will be used later for calculations, in the format that you have specified as your replacement to the default 'Date' format of your worksheet. If you don't, you might get unexpected results. For example, let us assume that you have used the command **/Worksheet, Global, Default, Other, International, Date** to choose your preferred type of date as dd/mm/yy. Should you then attempt to enter a date in the dd.mm.yy format, 1-2-3 will bleep and refuse to accept the entry. However, if you enter a date in dd-mm-yy format, 1-2-3 does not warn you, but fills the cell with asterisks instead. Furthermore, let us assume that you are entering information on a special screen under a macro control; you will certainly not notice the asterisks. Any further date arithmetic involving this cell will give incorrect results.

To illustrate the above point, amend the date in cell A:D4 of INVOICE4 to 10-4-92, then move to sheet B and issue the **/Data, Query, Extract** command. The result is shown below.

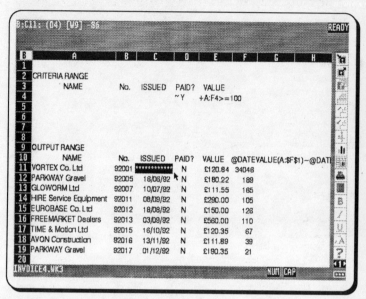

If you have changed the default 'date' format, make sure that you use the **Update** command (three levels back from choosing the date type) to make such choice permanent.

7. MACRO PRINCIPLES AND DESIGN

A macro is a set of instructions, made up of a sequence of keystrokes and commands, that you would normally have typed onto the keyboard, but which you type instead into a macro range, where it is stored for future use. After entering a macro, and allocating a keystroke sequence to it, it can be invoked by simply pressing those keys. Thus, a macro is a list of commands which is used to perform a specific task, and can be used whenever you wish to save time in performing repetitive commands.

At first glance the principle of macros may seem too complicated to a new 1-2-3 user, but their use adds enormously to the tasks possible with the package. Initially, to help with repetitive keystroke operations, but with more experience, macros can be used to customise the way 1-2-3 works. Very experienced 1-2-3 programmers use the advanced macro language to prepare separate applications which need not look anything like 1-2-3.

Creating a Macro

No matter how complicated a macro is, the process of both generating it and then using it, follows the same basic steps:

1. Enter keystroke sequences, or macro commands, onto a worksheet
2. Enter the macro name in the column to the left
3. Assign the name to the macro with the /**Range, Name, Labels, Right** command
4. Run the macro by invoking its name.

We will now use the spreadsheet saved as PROJECT1 (see chapter 2), to show how we can add macros to it, to perform 'what-if' type projections by, say, increasing the 'Wages' bill by 15%.

If you haven't saved PROJECT1 on disc, it will be necessary for you to enter the information shown on the next page so that you can benefit from what is to be introduced. Having done this, save it under PROJECT1 before going on.

If you have previously saved PROJECT1, then enter 1-2-3 and load the file. What should appear on screen is shown on the next page, but with the column widths adjusted.

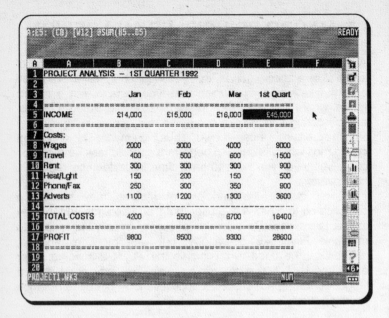

As an example we will 'Edit' the entries under 'Wages' so that this part of the costs can be increased by 15%. One way of doing this would be to multiply the contents of each cell containing the 'wages' value by 1.15. The exact steps, after highlighting cell B8, would be:

Manual Procedure	Equivalent Macro Steps
Press F2 to EDIT cell	{EDIT}
Type '*1.15'	*1.15
<Enter>	~
Press Right arrow	{RIGHT}

A full list of macro key names has been placed at the end of the chapter. Macros should be entered in their own worksheet in columnar fashion. Each command could be entered in a different row cell of the column, but the macro is easier to follow if a number of related commands are combined.

Use the /**Worksheet, Insert, Sheet, After** command to generate an empty worksheet on which to store macros. You could also place your macros in a separate file which would enable them to be used with any of your other files.

The important point, at this stage, is to keep your macros away from other data, so that they will not be corrupted by any editing of the data.

A good spreadsheet design, using the 3-dimensional ability of 1-2-3 could be as follows:

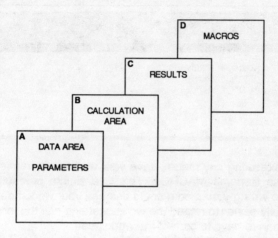

Type into cell B:B3 the combined macro commands

{EDIT}*1.15~{RIGHT}

and since each of the three months are to be changed, copy this entry to the two rows immediately below B3.

Having entered this simplistic macro, we now need to name it. 1-2-3 macros have two types of names, depending on how they are to be activated. Simple macros can have single letter names, such as \A. This type of macro would be activated by simply pressing the Alt+A keys whenever it was needed. A macro can, however, be given a full name of up to 15 characters long. To activate this type, press the RUN key (Alt+F3), type the full macro name, (or press NAME (F3) twice and highlight the macro name) and press <Enter>.

At this stage we will stick to simple macros and will only use the former method, so we will call our example macro \C (for percent): Type

^\C

into cell B:A3 and with the cursor in that cell type /**Range, Name, Labels, Right** followed by <Enter>. This gives the first cell of the macro column the name that was contained in the highlighted cell, (in our case \C).

Your screen should now display the following information:

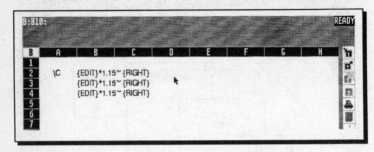

Before executing any macro, save your worksheet, in this case under the filename MACRO1. This is a simple precaution, if things go wrong your macro could damage your worksheet, and it is usually easier to reload the worksheet and edit the incorrect macro than to have to correct the worksheet!

To use this macro, highlight the first cell to be updated (in this case A:B8) and press Alt+C. Watch the changes that take place in the 'Wages' cell range A:B8..A:D8 as a result of the three line macro (an empty row signifies the end of a macro), and beyond to A:E8, as its contents depend on those of the Wages range.

We could use the same macro to increase the other costs by a different percentage, by editing it, but this would be rather inefficient. A better method is to allocate a cell for the % increase, say cell A:H8, and edit the macro so that reference to that cell is made in absolute terms. For example, in cell A:G8, type

Incr

and in cell A:H8 type the actual % increase (in the previous case this would have been 1.15). Change the macro first line to:

{EDIT}*$A:$H$8~{RIGHT}

copy it to the two rows below, re-type the original values in cells A:B8..A:D8, then highlight cell A:B8 and finally, press Alt+C.

The display should change to the one below, which shows part of a perspective view of the worksheet MACRO1.WK3.

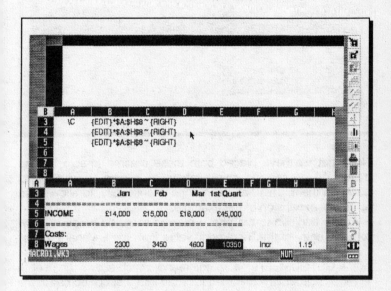

Now change the value in cell A:H8 to 1.20, to attempt to further increase the recently increased values in A:B8..A:D8 by an additional 20%.

You will notice in fact, that as soon as you change the contents of A:H8, the actual values in cells A:B8..A:D8 also change to reflect this new change. This, of course, will inevitably lead to errors, unless you incorporate the command **/Range, Value** within an additional macro, which should be executed prior to any attempt to change the contents of A:H8. This command changes a formula in a cell, to its current value. In other words it 'locks' the cell contents. Such a macro could incorporate the following commands:

/RVCosts~Costs~

where 'Costs' was defined as the range name for the cell block A:B8..A:D13. Implement this on row 1 of the macro worksheet, name it \V and save the resulting worksheet under the name MACRO2.

What you should have on your screen, is the following display:

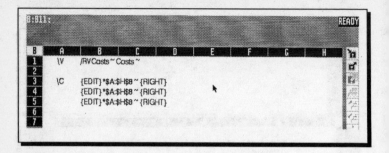

Note that we have placed both these macros (macro \C and macro \V) on specific row numbers of column B, with a gap between them. This has been done intentionally, to allow room for future expansion of the example.

A final addition to the above macros could be made to allow for user entry of the 'increment' value from the keyboard, rather than having to edit cell A:H8. This can be achieved by the use of the GETNUMBER macro command, which allows the user to enter a number which is then inserted into a specified cell in the worksheet. The general format of this macro command is:

{GETNUMBER prompt-string,location}

Other available macro commands are listed in Appendix E. In our particular case, the GETNUMBER command takes the following form:

{GETNUMBER "Enter increment ",A:H7}~

which is typed into cell B:B2. Don't forget to use the /**Range, Name** command to name macro \V. Save the resulting worksheet under the filename MACRO3, before using it. Your macro should now resemble the one on the screen dump shown on the next page.

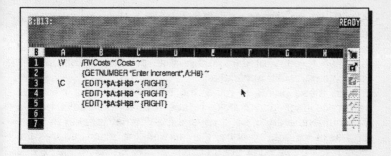

Finally, as an example of a macro which incorporates range names and an error routine, the file MACRO3 has been amended as shown below.

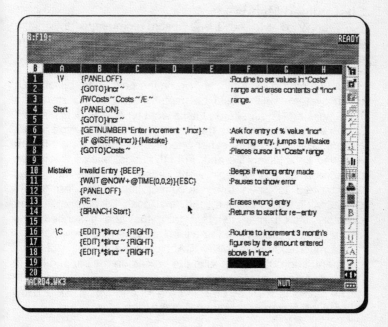

Error Checking:

When writing macros it is a good idea to use range names throughout. This allows you to change the location of data referenced by the macro, without having to keep track of, and change, cell addresses.

Also, a macro should be written in such a way as to anticipate any mistakes that might be made by the user. This requires error checking to be incorporated into it, that provides for the possible re-entry of data, rather than causing an abrupt exit from the particular application.

With these points in mind, the next macro uses the range reference 'Incr' and checks to see if an error results from a non-numeric entry. If so, it causes the internal speaker to bleep and asks for data re-entry. If all is well, the macro causes the cursor to be placed at the beginning of the 'Costs' range so that you can choose which of the various cost categories to update by activating macro \C. Before you run the amended macro, save it under the filename MACRO4.

Customised Menus

1-2-3 provides two advanced macro commands to enable customised menus to be built into your macros. These are particularly useful if you are designing applications for inexperienced users.

Our last macro example, shown on the next page, builds up a menu system which could be usefully used at the start of a 1-2-3 session. The first menu asks what type of work is planned for the session and makes the directory holding that type of files current. The sub-menu, either opens and names a new file, or retrieves an existing file and, in both cases, places the file on the screen for you to begin work. Before using the macro you would need to open three subdirectories under the 123R3 directory, 'Calcs', 'Memos' and 'Invoices'. Of course, if your directory structure is different from the one described, you would need to modify the three path statements on row 6.

The macro uses the {MENUCALL} command, which displays the menu subroutine named in the braces on the second line of the control panel at the top of the screen.

The macro is RUN by pressing Alt+**F3** and typing 'Start'. Row 1 holds the first menu command in the form

    {MENUCALL Menu1}

which displays the customised menu held in the subroutine 'Menu1'. If a selection is made other than a valid menu option, the computer bleeps in frustration!

	A	B	C	D	E
1	Start	{MENUCALL Menu1}			
2		{BEEP}{BRANCH Start}			
3					
4	Menu1	Calcs	Memos	Invoices	Quit
5		General calculations	Prepare memos	Work on invoices	Return to READY mode
6		/fd{CE}c:\123r34\Calcs~	/fd{CE}c:\123r34\Memos~	/fd{CE}c:\123r34\Invoices~	{QUIT}
7		{BRANCH Next}	{BRANCH Next}	{BRANCH Next}	
8					
9	Next	{MENUCALL Menu2}			
10		{BEEP}{BRANCH Next}			
11					
12	Menu2	New	Existing	Return	Quit
13		Open a New File	Open an Existing File	Previous Menu	Exit from Menu System
14		{Newname}	{BRANCH Get}	{BRANCH Start}	{QUIT}
15					
16	Newname	{GETLABEL "New File Name? ",New-nm}~			
17	New-nm	/fnb{CE}			
18					
19		~{QUIT}			
20					
21	Get	/fob{?}~			
22		{QUIT}			

93

A menu subroutine always has three parts. The first line must hold the items to be displayed on the menu line, preferably as single word options. On the second line, immediately below each menu item, a description message is placed. This is the message that will be placed under the menu line, when each menu item is highlighted. In our example these messages have been kept short so that the whole macro can be displayed on one page. In your applications the message can be much longer. On the third line and below are placed the macro commands for each menu item. These must be kept in the same column as the menu item they refer to. For clarity, it is often better to use the {BRANCH} command and place long lists of instructions in subroutines.

The MENUCALL command returns control to the line immediately below the MENUCALL statement once the menu instructions have been carried out. This command is used when you need to return to the menu to select further options. To enable an exit from the menu system, escape options should always be built in to each level. Hence the 'Quit' options in our example. The other menu command MENUBRANCH, returns control to the READY mode as soon as a set of menu instructions have been completed.

The example shows how you can build up a system of sub-menus. Once you have worked out what operations the various commands perform, it would be an easy matter to modify this macro to suit your own working system. Unfortunately if you are using a mouse with Release 3.x it will not function in macro menus, so you will have to revert to the keyboard.

Autoexecute Macros:
1-2-3 allows you to set one macro in a file to be run automatically as soon as the file is opened, or retrieved into memory. Such an 'autoexecute' macro must always be given the name /0 (zero). This only works if the

/Worksheet, Global, Default, Autoexec

setting is Yes, but as this is the default you will probably not have to worry about it. This facility could be used to make our menu macro operate every time 1-2-3 was used.

94

To do this, the Start routine in cell A1 should be renamed /0 and the file containing the macro should be loaded into memory on start up. With Release 3,4, 1-2-3 now has the facility of naming a file to be automatically loaded on start up. The file to be loaded must be named **auto123.wk3** and must be placed in the default working directory (the directory specified with the **/Worksheet, Global, Default, Dir** command.

Record Mode

So far, all our macro commands and keystrokes have been manually entered, but 1-2-3 provides an easy method of entering repetitive, keystroke type, macros into a worksheet with the 'Record Mode'. The RECORD key (Alt+**F2**) gives access to the 'record buffer' which stores all keystrokes, in a macro format, in a 512 byte section of memory.

When you want to record a macro, locate the pointer, press RECORD (Alt+**F2**) and select **Erase** to empty the buffer. Then carry out all the steps you want to automate in the eventual macro. To stop recording, press RECORD again, but this time follow it with **Copy**. The contents of the buffer are displayed in the control panel and 1-2-3 is put in EDIT mode. At this stage you can edit the buffer contents, if this is necessary. Select which contents you want to copy, using the <Tab> key as the pointer anchor, press <Enter> and specify the range to copy to. You should now have a set of macro instructions, but they will not be formatted in any meaningful way, just a series of commands which may be difficult to follow at some stage in the future.

The RECORD mode can also be used to repeat a series of keystrokes immediately, without actually generating a macro. The initial procedure to do this is the same, but after RECORD is pressed the second time (to stop recording), select 'Playback' from the menu. Once the desired keystrokes have been selected, press <Enter> to cause 1-2-3 to repeat them again.

Debugging a Macro:

Writing macros can lead to mistakes which you must find and correct. To help you with this task, 1-2-3 provides the STEP mode which allows you to check the execution of your macro one step at a time. Using this technique, you can see exactly what the macro is doing and where it is going wrong.

To invoke the STEP mode, press the RECORD key (Alt+F2) and select Step. The status indicator at the bottom of the worksheet will display the word STEP. If a macro is now invoked, the status indicator will indicate the current cell address and the contents of the macro command line being executed with the next keystroke instruction highlighted. You can now step through the macro one instruction at a time, by pressing the spacebar, and watch the results of each macro command. Once the error is found stop the macro by pressing <Ctrl+Break>, followed by <Esc>, and edit it in the normal manner. To turn off the STEP mode press RECORD, when 1-2-3 is in the READY mode, and select Step again.

Macro Keys

Most keystrokes can be manually entered in a macro by typing the appropriate key. All the special macro keys must be typed, as shown in the list below, enclosed in braces. You can use upper or lower-case letters when entering the special key names, but we recommend you make a habit of using upper-case. As a short cut you can type the left brace ({) and press NAME (F3), which produces a list of all 1-2-3's key names and advanced macro instructions. Simply highlight the instruction required and press <Enter>.

1-2-3 Key	*Macro Instruction*
↓	{DOWN} or {D}
←	{LEFT} or {L}
→	{RIGHT} or {R}
↑	{UP} or {U}
ABS (F4)	{ABS}
ADDIN (ALT+F10)	{ADDIN} or {APP4}
APP1 (ALT+F7)	{APP1}
APP2 (ALT+F8)	{APP2}
APP3 (ALT+F9)	{APP3}
BACKSPACE	{BACKSPACE} or {BS}
BIG LEFT <Ctrl+←>	{BIGLEFT}
BIG RIGHT <Ctrl+→>	{BIGRIGHT}
CALC (F9)	{CALC}

DEL	{DELETE} or {DEL}
EDIT (F2)	{EDIT}
END	{END}
ENTER	~
ESC	{ESCAPE} or {ESC}
FILE <Ctrl+End>	{FILE}
FIRST CELL <Ctrl+Home>	{FIRSTCELL} or {FC}
FIRST FILE <Ctrl+End Home>	{FIRSTFILE} or {FF} or {FILE} {HOME}
GOTO (F5)	{GOTO}
GRAPH (F10)	{GRAPH}
HELP (F1)	{HELP}
HOME	{HOME}
INS	{INSERT} or {INS}
LAST CELL <End Ctrl+Home>	{LASTCELL} or {LC}
LAST FILE <Ctrl+End End>	{LASTFILE} or {LF} or {FILE END}
NAME (F3)	{NAME}
NEXT FILE <Ctrl+End Ctrl+PgUp>	{NEXTFILE} or {NF} or {FILE} {NS}
NEXT SHEET <Ctrl+PgUp>	{NEXTSHEET or {NS}
PGUP	{PGUP}
PGDN	{PGDN}
PREV FILE <Ctrl+End Ctrl+PgDn>	{PREVFILE} or {PF} or {FILE} {PS}
PREV SHEET <Ctrl+PgDn>	{PREVSHEET} or {PS}
QUERY (F7)	{QUERY}
TABLE (F8)	{TABLE}
WINDOW (F6)	{WINDOW}
ZOOM (Alt+F6)	{ZOOM}
/ (or <)	{MENU} or / or <
~ (tilde)	{~}
{ (open brace)	{{}
} (close brace)	{}}

To specify two or more consecutive uses of the same key, use a repetition factor within the braces. For example,

{RIGHT 2} or {R2}, causes the cell pointer to move right twice.

{CE} Keystroke Instruction:

One extra instruction has been included with 1-2-3 Release 3.x which has no keyboard alternative. This is the {CLEARENTRY}, or {CE}, instruction which completely clears the edit line, unlike {ESC} which can take several attempts to accomplish this. Also, unlike {ESC}, it does not step back one command level if activated when the edit line is empty. This command is invaluable for clearing the default entries, automatically placed in the edit line, in macros that retrieve or open files.

* * *

1-2-3 has many more commands and functions, than those demonstrated, which can be used to build and run your application in special ways. What this book has tried to do is to introduce you to the overall subject and provide a solid foundation on which to build future knowledge.

* * *

APPENDIX A - INDICATORS

Indicators are highlighted words that appear either in the top right-hand corner of 1-2-3's control panel, or at the bottom of the screen, There are two types of indicators: Mode and Status.

Mode Indicators:

Mode indicators appear during every operation of 1-2-3 at the top right-hand corner of the screen. They inform the user of the current state or condition of 1-2-3's operation. The table below lists all the mode indicators with their associated description. The macro command {INDICATE} creates special indicators which are displayed in the same way.

Indicator	Description
EDIT	The current entry is being edited or needs to be edited
ERROR	An error has occurred. Press HELP (F1) to display a help screen, or to clear it, press <Esc> or <Enter>
FILES	A list of files is being displayed
FIND	A /**Data, Query, Find** operation is in progress
HELP	The help facility has been invoked
LABEL	A label is being entered
MENU	A command menu is being displayed
NAMES	A menu of existing range names, graph names, print setting names or @function names is being displayed
POINT	The highlighted bar is pointing to a cell or a range of cells
READY	1-2-3 is ready to receive data or a command
STAT	A status screen is being displayed
VALUE	A number or formula is being entered
WAIT	A command or process is being executed.
WYSIWYG	The Wysiwyg menu is currently active

Status Indicators:

Status indicators appear on the bottom status line of the screen and inform the user of the status of the program or of a key. For example, CALC indicates that the worksheet's formulae need to be recalculated, while CAP indicates that the <Caps Lock> key is on. The table below lists all the status indicators and gives their description.

Indicator	Description
CALC	If blue - the worksheet's formulae need to be recalculated; press the CALC key (**F9**). If red - a background calculation is taking place
CAP	The <Caps Lock> key is on
CIRC	The worksheet contains a formula that refers to itself. To locate the formula use the **/Worksheet, Status** command
CMD	A macro is being run
END	The <End> key has been pressed
FILE	The FILE key <Ctrl+End> has been pressed to move between files
GROUP	The current file is in GROUP mode
MEM	Less than 32KB of memory is available
NUM	The <NumLock> key is active
OVR	The overstrike mode is on; press the <Ins> key to return to INSERT mode
PRT	Program is printing to a printer or file
RO	The status of the current file is read-only
SCROLL	The <Scroll Lock> key is on
STEP	The STEP mode has been activated from the RECORD key (Alt+**F2**)
ZOOM	The ZOOM key (Alt+**F6**) has been pressed to give a full screen view.

APPENDIX B - @FUNCTIONS

Lotus 1-2-3's @functions are built-in formulae that perform specialised calculations. Their general format is:

@name(arg1,arg2,...)

where 'name' is the function name, and 'arg1', 'arg2', etc., are the arguments required for the evaluation of the function. Arguments must appear in a parenthesized list as shown above and their exact number depends on the function being used. However, there are eight functions that do not require arguments and are used without parentheses. These are: @ERR, @FALSE, @NA, @NOW, @PI, @RAND, @TODAY and @TRUE.

There are four types of arguments used with @functions: numeric values, range values, string values and conditions, the type used being dependent on the type of function. Numeric value arguments can be entered either directly as numbers, as a cell address, a cell range name or as a formula. Range value arguments can be entered either as a range address or a range name, while string value arguments can be entered as an actual value (a string in double quotes), as a cell address, a cell name, or a formula. Condition arguments normally use logical operators or refer to an address containing a logic formula.

Types of Functions

There are several types of functions, such as mathematical, logical, financial, statistical, string, date and time, special, and database. Each type requires its own number and type of arguments. These are listed below under the various function categories.

Mathematical Functions:

Mathematical functions evaluate a result using numeric arguments. The various functions and their meanings are as follows:

Function	Description
@ABS(X)	Returns the absolute value of X
@ACOS(X)	Returns the angle in radians, whose cosine is X (arc cos of X)

@ASIN(X)	Returns the angle in radians, whose sine is X (arc sin of X)
@ATAN(X)	Returns the angle in radians, between $\pi/2$ and $-\pi/2$, whose tangent is X (arc tan of X - 2 quadrant)
@ATAN2(X,Y)	Returns the angle in radians, between π and $-\pi$, whose tangent is Y/X (arc tan of Y/X - 4 quadrant)
@COS(X)	Returns the cosine of angle X (X must be in radians)
@EXP(X)	Raises e to the power of X
@INT(X)	Returns the integer part of X
@LN(X)	Returns the natural logarithm (base e) of X
@LOG(X)	Returns logarithm (base 10) of X
@MOD(X,Y)	Returns the remainder of X/Y
@PI	Returns the value of π (3.1415926)
@RAND	Returns a random number between 0 and 1
@ROUND(X,N)	Returns the value of X rounded to N places
@SIN(x)	Returns the sine of angle X (X must be in radians)
@SQRT(X)	Returns the square root of X
@TAN(X)	Returns the tangent of angle X (X must be in radians).

Logical Functions:

Logical functions produce a value based on the result of a conditional statement, using numeric arguments. The various functions and their meanings are as follows:

Function	*Description*
@FALSE	Returns the logical value 0
@IF(Cr,X,Y)	Returns the value X if Cr is TRUE and Y if Cr is FALSE
@ISERR(X)	Returns 1 (TRUE) if X contains ERR, else returns 0 (FALSE)
@ISNA(X)	Returns 1 (TRUE) if X contains NA, else returns 0 (FALSE)

102

@ISNUMBER(X)	Returns 1 (TRUE) if X contains a numeric value, else returns 0 (FALSE)
@ISRANGE(Rg)	Returns 1 (TRUE) if Rg is a defined range or valid cell address, else returns 0 (FALSE)
@ISSTRING(X)	Returns 1 (TRUE) if X contains a string value, else returns 0 (FALSE)
@TRUE	Returns the logical value 1.

Financial Functions:

Financial functions evaluate loans, annuities, depreciation and cash flows over a period of time, using numeric arguments. Percentages should be entered either as a decimal (for example, 0.155) or with a percent sign (for example, 15.5%). The various functions and their meanings are as follows:

Function	*Description*
@CTERM(Rt,Fv,Pv)	Returns the number of compounding periods for an investment of present value Pv, to grow to a future value Fv, at a fixed interest rate Rt
@DDB(Ct,Sg,Lf,Pd)	Returns the double-declining depreciation allowance of an asset, with original cost Ct, predicted salvage value Sg, life Lf, and period Pd
@FV(Pt,Rt,Tm)	Returns the future value of a series of equal payments, each of equal amount Pt, earning a periodic interest rate Rt, over a number of payment periods in term Tm
@IRR(Gs,Rg)	Returns the internal rate of return of the series of cash flows in a range Rg, based on the approximate percentage guess Gs
@NPV(Rt,Rg)	Returns the net present value of the series of future cash flows in range Rg, discounted at a periodic interest rate Rt

103

@PMT(Pl,Rt,Tm)	Returns the amount of the periodic payment needed to pay off the principal Pl, at a periodic interest rate Rt, over the number of payment periods in term Tm
@PV(Pt,Rt,Tm)	Returns the present value of a series of payments, each of equal amount Pt, discounted at a periodic interest rate Rt, over a number of payment periods in term Tm
@RATE(Fv,Pv,Tm)	Returns the periodic interest rate necessary for a present value Pv to grow to a future value Fv, over the number of compounding periods in term Tm
@SLN(Ct,Sg,Lf)	Returns the straight line depreciation allowance of an asset for one period, given the original cost Ct, predicted salvage value Sg, and the life Lf of the asset
@SYD(Ct,Sg,Lf,Pd)	Returns the sum-of-the-years' digits depreciation allowance of an asset, given the original cost Ct, predicted salvage value Sg, life Lf, and period Pd
@TERM(Pt,Rt,Fv)	Returns the number of payment periods of an investment, with amount of each payment Pt, the periodic interest rate Rt, and the future value of the investment Fv
@VDB(Ct,Sg,Lf,S,E,*d,s*)	Returns the depreciation allowance of an asset, of original cost Ct, salvage value Sg, life Lf, over a period from start S to end E. The arguments, depreciation-factor *d* and switch *s,* are optional. If *s* is set at 1 the function returns declining balance depreciation for life, else straight-line is used for the remaining period after E.

Statistical Functions:

Statistical functions evaluate lists of values using numeric arguments or cell ranges. The various functions and their meanings are as follows:

Function	Description
@AVG(Rg)	Returns the average of values in range Rg
@COUNT(Rg)	Returns the number of non-blank entries in range Rg
@MAX(Rg)	Returns the maximum value in range Rg
@MIN(Rg)	Returns the minimum value in range Rg
@STD(Rg)	Returns the population standard deviation of values in range Rg
@STDS(Rg)	Returns the sample standard deviation of values in range Rg
@SUM(Rg)	Returns the sum of values in range Rg
@SUMPRODUCT(Ls)	Returns the sum of the products of multiple ranges contained in the list Ls
@VAR(Rg)	Returns the population variance of values in range Rg
@VARS(Rg)	Returns the sample variance of values in range Rg.

String Functions:

String functions operate on strings and produce numeric or string values dependent on the function.

Function	Description
@CHAR(X)	Returns the LMBCS (Lotus Multibyte Character Set) character that corresponds to the code number X
@CODE(Sg)	Returns the LMBCS code number for the first character in string Sg
@EXACT(Sg1,Sg2)	Returns 1 (TRUE) if strings Sg1 and Sg2 are exactly alike, otherwise 0 (FALSE)

@FIND(Ss,Sg,Sn)	Returns position at which the first occurrence of search string Ss begins in string Sg, starting the search from search number Sn
@LEFT(Sg,N)	Returns the first (leftmost) N characters in string Sg
@LENGTH(Sg)	Returns the number of characters in string Sg
@LOWER(Sg)	Converts all the letters in string Sg to lowercase
@MID(Sg,Sn,N)	Returns N characters from string Sg beginning with the character at Sn
@N(Rg)	Returns the numeric value in the upper left corner cell in range Rg
@PROPER(Sg)	Converts all words in string Sg to first letter in uppercase and the rest in lowercase
@REPEAT(Sg,N)	Returns string Sg N times. Unlike the repeating character (\), the output is not limited by the column width
@REPLACE(O,S,N,Ns)	Removes N characters from original string O, starting at character S and then inserts new string Ns in the vacated place
@RIGHT(Sg,N)	Returns the last (rightmost) N characters in string Sg
@S(Rg)	Returns the string value in the upper left corner cell in range Rg
@STRING(X,N)	Returns the numeric value X as a string, with N decimal places
@TRIM(Sg)	Returns string Sg with no leading, trailing or consecutive spaces
@UPPER(Sg)	Converts all letters in string Sg to uppercase
@VALUE(Sg)	Returns the numeric value of string Sg.

Date and Time Functions:

Date and time functions generate and use serial numbers to represent dates and times. Each date between 1 January, 1900 and 31 December 2099 has an integer serial number starting with 1 and ending with 73050. Each moment during a day has a decimal serial number starting with 0.000 at midnight and ending with 0.99999 just before the following midnight. Thus the value 0.5 indicates midday. The various functions and their meanings are as follows:

Function	Description
@DATE(Yr,Mh,Dy)	Returns the date number of argument Yr,Mh,Dy
@DATEVALUE(Ds)	Returns the date number of date string Ds
@DAY(Dn)	Returns the day of the month number (1-31) of date number Dn
@D360(Sn,En)	Returns the number of days between dates Sn and En, based on a year of 12 months, each of 30 days
@HOUR(Tn)	Returns the hour number (0-23) of time number Tn
@MINUTE(Tn)	Returns the minute number (0-59) of time number Tn
@MONTH(Dn)	Returns the month number (1-12) of date number Dn
@NOW	Returns the serial number for the current date and time
@SECOND(Tn)	Returns the second number (0-59) of time number Tn
@TIME(Hr,Ms,Ss)	Returns the time number of argument Hr,Ms,Ss
@TIMEVALUE(Ts)	Returns the time number of time string Ts
@TODAY	Returns the current date number
@YEAR(Dn)	Returns the year number (0-199) of date number Dn.

Special Functions:

Special functions perform a variety of advanced tasks, such as looking up values in a table. The various functions and their meanings are as follows:

Function	Description
@?	Indicates an unknown @function from an add-in program
@(Ca)	Returns the contents of the cell referenced by cell address Ca
@CELL(At,Rg)	Returns the code representing the attribute At of range Rg
@CELLPOINTER(At)	Returns the code representing the attribute At of the highlighted cell
@CHOOSE(X,V0,..,Vn)	Returns the Xth value in the list V0,..,Vn
@COLS(Rg)	Returns the number of columns in the range Rg
@COORD(Wk,C,R,Ab)	Returns an address with values, worksheet Wk, column C, Row R; the address being absolute, relative or mixed depending on Ab
@ERR	Returns the value ERR
@HLOOKUP(X,Rg,Rn)	Performs a horizontal table look-up by comparing the value X to each cell in the top index row, in range Rg, then moves down the column in which a match is found by the specified row number Rn
@INDEX(Rg,Cn,Rw,[W])	Returns the value of the cell in range Rg at the intersection of column-offset Cn, row-offset Rw and worksheet-offset W; used to refer to a lookup table with relative positions rather than the specified values required by @HLOOKUP and @VLOOKUP
@INFO(At)	Returns system information based on the attribute At
@NA	Returns NA (not available)
@ROWS(Rg)	Counts the rows in range Rg

@SHEETS(Rg)	Counts the sheets in range Rg
@SOLVER(St)	Returns a value which gives information about the status of SOLVER
@VLOOKUP(X,Rg,Cn)	Performs a vertical table look-up by comparing the value X to each cell in the first index column, in range Rg, then moves across the row in which a match is found by the specified column number Cn.

Database Functions:

Database functions perform calculations on a database. The database, called the input range, consists of records, which include fields and field names, like Os below. A criterion range must be set up to select the records from the database that each function uses. The various functions and their meanings are as follows:

Function	Description
@DAVG(Ip,Os,Cr)	Returns the average of the values in the offset column Os, of the input range Ip that meet the criteria in the criterion range Cr
@DCOUNT(Ip,Os,Cr)	Returns the number of non-blank cells in the offset column Os, of the input range Ip that meet the criteria in the criterion range Cr
@DGET(Ip,Os,Cr)	Returns the value or label from field Os in the input range Ip that meets the criteria in the range Cr
@DMAX(Ip,Os,Cr)	Returns the maximum value in the offset column Os, of the input range Ip that meet the criteria in the criterion range Cr
@DMIN(Ip,Os,CR)	Returns the minimum value in the offset column Os, of the input range Ip that meet the criteria in the criterion range Cr
@DQUERY(Fn,Ex)	Sends a command Fn, with arguments Ex, to an external database management program

109

@DSTD(Ip,Os,Cr)	Returns the population standard deviation of the values in the offset column Os, of the input range Ip that meet the criteria in the criterion range Cr
@DSTDS(Ip,Os,Cr)	Returns the sample standard deviation of the values in the offset column Os, of the input range Ip that meet the criteria in the criterion range Cr
@DSUM(Ip,Os,Cr)	Returns the sum of the values in the offset column Os, of the input range Ip that meet the criteria in the criterion range Cr
@DVAR(Ip,Os,Cr)	Returns the population variance of the values in the offset column Os, of the input range Ip that meet the criteria in the criterion range Cr
@DVARS(Ip,Os,Cr)	Returns the sample variance of the values in the offset column Os, of the input range Ip that meet the criteria in the criterion range Cr.

APPENDIX C - SMARTICONS

The SmartIcons are grouped by function In numbered palettes from 2 to 8. Palette 1 is the custom palette that you can change to include all the icons you most often use by copying them from the other palettes. Therefore, we do not list the icons of Palette 1, as these might have been changed by the user and, in any case, are to be found in the other permanent palettes. Icons within a palette are numbered for easy reference.

Palette 2

 1   Saves the current worksheet file to a disc

 2   Adds or removes single underlining to data in a range

 3   Adds or removes double underlining to data in a range

 4   Formats values in a range as currency or restores global format

 5   Formats values in a range as comma format or restores global format

 6   Formats values in a range as percent or restores global format

 7   Cycles through available fonts for highlighted range

 8   Cycles through available colours for data in the highlighted range

 9   Cycles through available colours for background for the highlighted range

	10	Adds or removes a drop shadow and outline to a range
	11	Cycles through available outline styles for highlighted range
	12	Cycles through available shading styles for highlighted range
	13	Left-aligns labels in a range
	14	Centres labels in a range
	15	Right-aligns labels in a range
	16	Starts the 1-2-3 Help system.

Palette 3

	1	Saves the current worksheet file to a disc
	2	Inserts one or more rows above the highlighted rows
	3	Inserts one or more columns to the left of the highlighted columns
	4	Deletes all rows in the highlighted range
	5	Deletes all columns in the highlighted range

6 Inserts a new worksheet after the current worksheet

 7 Deletes selected worksheets

 8 Inserts a page break in the row containing the cell pointer

 9 Inserts a page break in the column containing the cell pointer

 10 Sorts a database in ascending order using current column as sort key

 11 Sorts a database in descending order using current column as sort key

 12 Fills the highlighted range with a sequence of values

 13 Recalculates all formulae in the worksheet

 14 Enters today's date in the current cell or uses current Date/Time format

 15 Changes the display size of the worksheet

 16 Starts the 1-2-3 Help system.

1 Saves the current worksheet file to a disc

 2 Moves the cell pointer left one cell

 3 Moves the cell pointer right one cell

 4 Moves the cell pointer up one cell

 5 Moves the cell pointer down one cell

 6 Moves the worksheet display one screen up

 7 Moves the worksheet display one screen down

 8 Moves the worksheet display one screen to the left

 9 Moves the worksheet display one screen to the right

 10 Moves the worksheet display one column to the left

 11 Moves the worksheet display one column to the right

 12 Moves the worksheet display one row up

 13 Moves the worksheet display one row down

14 Moves the cell pointer to upper left corner of the current worksheet

 15 Moves the cell pointer to lower right corner of the active area

 16 Starts the 1-2-3 Help system.

Palette 5

 1 Saves the current worksheet file to a disc

 2 Displays three worksheets in perspective mode

 3 Moves the cell pointer to the next worksheet

 4 Moves the cell pointer to the previous worksheet

 5 Moves cell pointer down to intersection of a blank and nonblank cell

 6 Moves cell pointer up to intersection of a blank and nonblank cell

 7 Moves cell pointer right to intersection of a blank and nonblank cell

 8 Moves cell pointer left to intersection of a blank and nonblank cell

 9 Lets you move the cell pointer to a cell you specify

10 Lets you find or replace characters in labels and formulae in a range

 11 Copies the highlighted range to a range you specify

 12 Moves the highlighted range to a range you specify

 13 Copies the Wysiwyg attributes of the current range to another range

 14 Cancels your previous action or command if the UNDO feature is on

 15 Erases the highlighted range

 16 Starts the 1-2-3 Help system.

Palette 6

 1 Saves the current worksheet file to a disc

 2 Replaces the current file with a file from disc

 3 Reads a file into memory after the current file

 4 Creates a new file after the current file

 5 Prints the current print range, or prints the highlighted range

6 Previews current print range, or specifies/previous highlighted range

 7 Sum values in range

 8 Sum values in the cells directly behind the current cell in a 3D-file

 9 Graphs contents of table or highlighted range, or displays current graph

 10 Adds the current graph to the worksheet

 11 Displays the current graph

 12 Edits text in a selected range

 13 Changes the way text is aligned across columns

 14 Circles highlighted cell or range

 15 Copies contents of current cell to each cell in the highlighted range

 16 Starts the 1-2-3 Help system.

Palette 7

 1 Saves the current worksheet file to a disc

 2 Displays data in a range in bold or clears bold from a range

 3 Displays data in a range in italics or clears italics from a range

 4 Clears all Wysiwyg formats from range, restores default font

 5 Turns on STEP mode, which executes macros one step at a time

 6 Lets you select and run a macro

 7 Adds an icon to your custom palette

 8 Removes an icon from your custom palette

 9 Lets you rearrange icons on your custom palette

 10 Lets you examine or define the user icons

 11 Starts the 1-2-3 Help system.

Palette 8

 to **UI2** User-defined icons.

APPENDIX D - OTHER ADD-INS

Apart from the Wysiwyg add-in, Lotus 1-2-3 Release 3.4 comes with four additional add-ins; the Auditor, the Backsolver, the Solver, and the Viewer. These are programs that you can run while using 1-2-3 to provide additional functionality, without having to leave the worksheet you are working on at the time. A short description of what these programs can do is given below.

Starting Add-Ins

Before you can use an add-in, you must have specified that you wanted to transfer the files of that particular add-in to your hard disc during the installation process, unless you are using 1-2-3 on a network. Even if you have specified during installation that an add-in should load automatically, you still have to 'invoke' it in order to use it.

To start an add-in, press **Alt+F10** (ADDIN) to display the add-in menu. Then select the **Load** command and specify the file to load into memory (add-in files have the .PLC extension), and choose 1, 2, or 3 to assign the add-in to the **Alt+F7**, **Alt+F8**, or **Alt+F9** function keys respectively, or choose No-Key if you don't want to assign a function key to the particular add-in.

To invoke an add-in, press its assigned function key, if you have assigned one to it, or if you have not, press **Alt+F10**, select **Invoke** from the add-in menu, and then specify the name of the add-in.

The Auditor Add-In

You use the Auditor to analyse the way your worksheet is structured, or for locating formulae in order to find the source of errors.

When you invoke Auditor, a menu and settings sheet is displayed informing you of the current audit range and audit mode. The audit range is the range that contains the formulae you want to analyse, the default being all worksheets in all files in memory. The audit mode allows you to choose whether the Auditor highlights, lists, or moves forward or backward through identified formulae, dependents, etc. This choice can be made through the **Options** command, but the default mode is to highlight.

The Auditor commands have the following functions:

Command	Function
Circs	Identifies all cells involved in a circular reference
Dependents	Identifies all formulae in the audit range that refer to a particular cell
Formulas	Identifies all formulae in the audit range
Options	Allows the alteration of the audit range and audit mode, or toggles these to their default settings
Precedents	Identifies all cells in the audit range that provide data for a particular formula
Recalc-List	Identifies all formulae in the order that 1-2-3 recalculates them.

The Backsolver Add-In

You use the Backsolver to fine-tune a formula that gives you the required result by changing one or more of the variables that affect the final value. To effectively use Backsolver, you must adhere to the following procedure:

- Type the formula to be fine-tuned by Backsolver in a cell and select the required result the formula is to give, and which variables in the formula should be changed.

- Invoke Backsolver, select **Formula-Cell** from its menu, and specify the address or range name of the cell that contains the formula you want to fine-tune.

- Select the **Value** menu option and specify the value you want the formula in the formula cell to equate to when Backsolver solves the problem - you can enter either a number or another formula.

- Select the **Adjust** menu option and specify the address or range name of the cells whose values Backsolver can change. If you don't want to lose the original values in these adjustable cells, then copy them on another part of the worksheet before starting Backsolver.

- Select the **Solve** menu option. If Backsolver finds an answer to the problem, it displays the new values in the adjustable cells, otherwise it tells you why it can't do it.

The Solver Add-In

You use the Solver if you want to analyse data in a worksheet and solve "what-if" type of problems. Solver is ideal for problems that have more than one answer. It can investigate different options and present you with alternative solutions, including the best match to your requirements.

To use Solver, you start with a worksheet model. Solver problems can be set up in one or more worksheet files in memory, by selecting which cells to adjust, adding logical formulae, and defining the limits of the required answers.

To start Solver, first invoke it and then use the following procedure:

- Select the **Define, Adjustable** command and specify the adjustable cells. These are cells that contain values that Solver can adjust when it searches for an answer.

- Select the **Constraints** command and specify the constraint cells. These are cells which contain the logical formulae that define the answers you want Solver to find. A logical formula is one that returns either 1 (TRUE) or 0 (FALSE), depending on whether a condition is satisfied. Only use a simple logical formula per constraint cell. For compound logical formulae, enter simple logical formulae across several cells.

- Select the **Optimal** command and choose **X Maximize** to find the highest value for the optimal cell or **N Minimize** to find the lowest value of the optimal cell. Next, specify the optimal cell.

- Select the **Solve, Problem** command.

After Solver finds the required answers, it displays the first answer (or attempted answer) in the worksheet. A progress message at the bottom of the screen tells you how many answers (or attempts) Solver has found. If you have specified an optimal cell, the first answer is the 'optimal' or 'best' answer.

If a problem is too complex, or contains unacceptable @functions (for a list of permissible @functions see your Reference manual), or any argument in the @function depends on an adjustable cell, or the contents of a constraint or optimal cell refer to the @function, Solver will display an error message.

The Viewer Add-In

You use the Viewer if you want to find a specific piece of work, but cannot remember which worksheet contains it. Viewer allows you to scan the contents of any worksheet without having to retrieve it.

To start Viewer, first invoke it which displays a menu of four commands. These commands and their function are listed below:

Command	*Function*
Retrieve	Allows you to view and retrieve a file with the extension .WK1, .WKS, .WR1, .WRK, or .WK3
Open	Allows you to view and open a file with the extension .WK1, .WKS, .WR1, .WRK, or .WK3, before or after
Link	Allows you to view and link a file with the extension .WK1, .WKS, .WR1, .WRK, or .WK3
Browse	Allows you to browse a list of files with the extension .WK1, .WKS, .WR1, .WRK, or .WK3

Selecting anyone of the above commands causes a split screen to be displayed. On the left of the screen appears a list of files which exist on the logged directory, while on the right of the screen the actual contents of the highlighted file on the list are displayed. On the bottom of the screen there is one line of information relating to the highlighted file, and below it appears the 'function key' bar from which you can change the order the files appear in the 'list window'. For example, you can choose between alphabetical order or in order by dates of creation.

Viewer recognises and displays several different types of files, including 1-2-3, Symphony, Lotus Works, and ASCII text files - Wysiwyg formatting is not displayed. Although Viewer tries to display the contents of any file you choose, some of these, such as the contents of executable files will not make much sense.

APPENDIX E - MACRO COMMANDS

There are a large number of advanced macro commands available in 1-2-3, each one of which has a specified syntax. This takes one of the following two forms:

{Keyword}
{Keyword arg1,arg2,...,argn}

and must be typed into a macro with the prescribed number of arguments. Uppercase and lowercase letters are equivalent in macro keywords and are, therefore, interchangeable. However, it is a good idea to always use a different case for macro commands from that of range names. In the examples given in this book, all macro commands are entered in uppercase, while range names are entered in lowercase. This makes it easier to distinguish between the two.

Note that incorrect macro commands result in an error when the macro is invoked, and not when the macro command is entered. Also, note that there is an important difference between macros and @functions. If you place your macros in any place other than their own worksheet or file, commands that disrupt the sheet layout, such as **/Move**, **/Worksheet, Insert**, or **/Worksheet, Delete**, may cause the macro to fail.

Some macro commands, such as GETNUMBER, change the contents of cells in the worksheet. However, with some macro commands 1-2-3 does not update or recalculate the worksheet after the command is executed, even if recalculation is set to AUTOMATIC. The inclusion of either a tilde (~), which executes an <Enter>, or the {CALC} instruction, as the next macro instruction, is necessary to force a recalculation of the worksheet.

In the following list, a superscripted C (^{C}) against a command indicates that a {CALC} command, or ~, must be used to force a recalculation. Optional arguments are placed in square brackets ([..])

?	{?} stops macro execution temporarily for keyboard input
APPENDBELOW	{APPENDBELOW Dest,Sour} copies the contents of Sour to the rows below Dest

APPENDRIGHT	{APPENDRIGHT Dest,Sour} copies the contents of Sour to the columns immediately to the right of Dest
BEEP	{BEEP [Num]} causes the speaker to beep. Num is an optional number from 1 to 4 used for different tones (the default value is 1)
BLANK	{BLANK Loc} erases the contents of a specified cell location given by Loc or a range of cells such as A1..A9
BORDERSOFF	{BORDERSOFF} works the same as {FRAMEOFF}
BORDERSON	{BORDERSON} works the same as {FRAMEON}
BRANCH	{BRANCH Loc} causes macro execution to branch to a different location
BREAK	{BREAK} clears the control panel contents and returns 1-2-3 to READY mode
BREAKOFF	{BREAKOFF} disables the <Ctrl+Break> key during macro execution
BREAKON	{BREAKON} enables the <Ctrl+Break> key function
CE	{CE} or {CLEARENTRY} clears the default entry shown in the edit line of the control panel
CLOSE	{CLOSE} closes a file that has been opened with the OPEN command
CONTENTS[c]	{CONTENTS Dest,Sour,[Wdth],[Frmt]} places the contents of Source cell, if a 'string', into Destination cell as a label. If the contents of the Source cell are numeric and the *optional* arguments of Width and Format are different from those of the Source cell, then 1-2-3 takes the number in Source together with specified Width and Format and stores it as a left-aligned label in Destination cell

DEFINE[c]	{DEFINE Loc1:Type1,Loc2:Type2,Loc..} specifies Location cells and declares Types of arguments to be passed to a subroutine
DISPATCH	{DISPATCH Loc} branches indirectly to the specified destination, given by Loc
FILESIZE[c]	{FILESIZE Loc} determines the number of bytes in a currently opened file and places it in a specified Location
FOR[c]	{FOR Count,Start,Stop,Step,Startloc} executes repeatedly the macro subroutine that begins at the Start location. Count is a cell in which 1-2-3 holds the current number of repetition, while Startloc is the first cell, or range name of which subroutine to be executed
FORBREAK	{FORBREAK} cancels execution of current FOR loop
FORM	{FORM InputLoc,[Call],[IList],[EList]} suspends macro operation to enable editing of InputLoc. The optional parameters allow close control of the input
FORMBREAK	{FORMBREAK} ends a {FORM} command
FRAMEOFF	{FRAMEOFF} turns off the display of the worksheet frame
FRAMEON	{FRAMEON} turns on the display of the worksheet frame
GET[c]	{GET Loc} stops macro execution temporarily and stores a single character you type in a specified cell given by Loc
GETLABEL[c]	{GETLABEL Prompt,Loc} stops macro execution temporarily, prompts you with Prompt string and stores the characters you type as a label in a specified cell given by Loc
GETNUMBER[c]	{GETNUMBER Prompt,Loc} stops macro execution temporarily, prompts you with Prompt string and stores the characters you type as a number in a specified cell given by Loc

GETPOS[c]

{GETPOS Loc} determines the current position of the file pointer in an open file and displays it in Loc

GRAPHOFF

{GRAPHOFF} removes a graph displayed by {GRAPHON} and re-displays the worksheet

GRAPHON

{GRAPHON [Na],[Nodis]} displays: with no arguments the current graph, the graph named Na, or no graph display but makes Na current

IF

{IF Cond} executes the command that follows, in the same cell, if Cond is true, else moves control to next line down

INDICATE

{INDICATE [String]} shows String as the mode indicator

LET[c]

{LET Loc,String} stores an entered label or {LET Loc,Num} stores an entered number, in a specified cell given by Loc

LOOK[c]

{LOOK Loc} scans the keyboard for input during macro execution and stores that character in Loc

MENUBRANCH

{MENUBRANCH Loc} stops execution of a macro to allow selection from a customised menu with user-defined choices. The upper left-corner of the menu is given by Loc

MENUCALL

{MENUCALL Loc} stops macro execution to allow menu selection and executes the corresponding macro as a subroutine. The upper left-corner of the menu is given by Loc

ONERROR[c]

{ONERROR Loc,[Msg]} branches to Loc if an error occurs during macro execution. The error message can be optionally recorded at location Msg

OPEN

{OPEN Filename,Mode} opens the specified file in the current directory for reading or writing. Mode is a single character (R for Read, W for Write, M for Modify, or A for Append) which describes the type of file access

PANELOFF	{PANELOFF [Clear]} freezes the control panel during macro operation. If optional Clear is set the panel is also cleared
PANELON	{PANELON} enables control panel redrawing
PUT^c	{PUT Loc,Col,Row,String} puts a string or {PUT Loc,Col,Row,Num} puts a number, in the specified Location within a specified range
QUIT	{QUIT} terminates macro execution and returns control to the keyboard
READ^c	{READ Bytes,Loc} reads a number of bytes (characters) from a file into a cell specified by Loc
READLN^c	{READLN Loc} copies a line of characters from the currently open file into the specified location
RECALC	{RECALC Loc,[Condit],[Iternum]} recalculates the formulae in a specified range, row by row. Condit and Iternum are optional arguments; Condit is evaluated after the range Location is calculated and if Condit is FALSE, it calculates the range again; Iternum specifies the number of times the range is calculated
RECALCCOL	{RECALCCOL Loc,[Condit],[Iternum]} recalculates the formulae in a specified range a specified range, column by column under the same conditions as RECALC
RESTART	{RESTART} cancels the subroutine and clears the subroutine stack
RETURN	{RETURN} returns from a subroutine
SETPOS	{SETPOS Pointer} sets the file Pointer in the currently opened file into a new position
SYSTEM	{SYSTEM Cmd} halts 1-2-3 session to execute DOS command Cmd, then macro continues
WAIT	{WAIT Timenum} suspends macro execution for a specified time

WINDOWSOFF	{WINDOWSOFF} disables redrawing the display screen during macro execution
WINDOWSON	{WINDOWSON} enables normal screen redrawing
WRITE	{WRITE String} copies String into the open text file
WRITELN	{WRITELN String} adds String, plus a carriage return and line-feed sequence, to the open text file.

INDEX

NOTES

NOTES

NOTES

NOTES

NOTES

NOTES

COMPANION DISC TO THIS BOOK

This book contains many pages of file/program listings. There is no reason why you should spend many hours typing them into your computer, unless you wish to do so or need the practice.

The COMPANION DISC for this book comes with all the listings, organised into a separate subdirectory for each chapter. It is available in both 3.5-inch and 5.25-inch formats.

COMPANION DISCS for all books written by the same author(s) and published by BERNARD BABANI (publishing) LTD, are also available and are listed at the front of this book. Make sure you specify the BP book number and the book title in your order.

ORDERING INSTRUCTIONS

To obtain your copy of the disc companion, fill-in the order form below, enclose a cheque (payable to **P.R.M. Oliver**) or a postal order, and send it to the address given below.

Book No.	Book Name	Unit Price	Total Price
BP ___		£2.50	
BP ___		£2.50	
BP ___		£2.50	
Name .... Address .... Disc Format 3.5-inch....... 5.25-inch.......		Sub-total P & P Total Due	£............. £.... 0.45 £.............
Send to: P.R.M. Oliver, CSM, Pool, Redruth, Cornwall, TR15 3SE			